THE DESTRUCTION OF MODERN JERUSALEM

By
Willie M. Manipol

ISBN-13: 978-1-57258-546-1
ISBN-13: 1-57258-546-3
Library of Congress Control Number: 2008937079

The Destruction of Modern Jerusalem is a compilation of Bible and Spirit of Prophecy quotations that are relevant to the issues facing modern Jerusalem/Israel of today—the Seventh-day Adventist church. It is hoped that this humble work will awaken the ten virgins in the church when the final loud cry is given. "And at midnight there was a cry made, Behold, the bridegroom cometh; go ye out to meet him." (Matthew 25:6)

Willie M. Manipol

Present Truth Global Ministries
Glendale, CA 91205
Email:ptgm7@yahoo.com

CONTENTS

PREFACE

Jesus Christ prophecy recorded in Matthew 24:15-22 is a dire and urgent warning to every faithful follower of our Lord and Saviour Jesus Christ, and should be studied diligently. It is a vivid portrayal of an end time event that will occur just before His second coming. The first application of the prophecy happened thirty-nine years later after His pronouncement to ancient Jerusalem/Israel. The second and final application of prophecy points to His end time people—modern Jerusalem/Israel.

The parallelism between ancient Jerusalem/Israel and modern Jerusalem/Israel is quite startling and even thought provoking. Most Seventh-day Adventists are unaware of the fact that we are exactly following the footsteps of ancient Jerusalem/Israel. *"That which has been, will be, except that the* ***coming struggle will be marked with a terrible intensity*** *such as the world has never witnessed."* **The Seventh-day Adventist church is God's modern Jerusalem/Israel** as confirmed by the writings of Ellen G. White—God's last day messenger to the remnant church. We are living in the most solemn period of this earth's history, the "Day of Atonement."

Had it not been for the blessing of the inspired writings of Ellen G. White—the Spirit of Prophecy, we will never come to the realization and clear understanding of end time Bible prophecies. The gift of prophecy—*one of the choicest of all the gifts of the Spirit, [Life Sketches, p. 468]* was solely given to His last day church, as in the "Day of Pentecost." The Bible and Spirit of Prophecy are to be our guide to prepare our characters for the soon coming of Jesus Christ. We have to be sealed with **"present sealing truth"** before the time of trouble such as never was since the foundation of the world.

"The Lord has shown me that precious souls are ***starving, and dying for want of present sealing truth, the meat in due season;*** *and the swift messengers should speed*

on their way, and feed the flock with **present truth**. *I heard an Angel say, 'speed the swift messengers, speed the swift messengers; for the case of every soul will soon be decided, either for life or death." —Review & Herald, vol. 1, p. 11*

In the closing work of the gospel, the eleventh hour workers will proclaim the three angels' messages of Revelation 12:17, 19:10, 14:6-12, 18:1-5. They will stand in defense of the Bible Sabbath truth when the whole world have made it void through legislation. —Exodus 20:8-11, 31:13; Ezekiel 20:12, 20; Ecclesiastes 12:13-14. Those who keep the commandments of God and the faith of Jesus—God's remnant, will develop a Christ-like character through long persevering effort, sore discipline, stern conflict and lifelong obedience. These will compose the elect of God, the one hundred forty-four thousand.

"Let me tell you that the Lord will work in this last work in a manner very much out of the common order of things, and in a way that will be contrary to any human planning. There will be those among us who will always want to control the work of God, to dictate even what movements shall be made when the work goes forward under the direction of the angel who joins the third angel in the message to be given to the world. ***God will use ways and means by which it will be seen that He is taking the reins in His own hands****. The workers will be surprised by the simple means that He will use to bring about and perfect His work of righteousness." —Testimonies to Ministers, p. 300*

The first chapter of this book, the Destruction of Jerusalem, is the 1884 original edition of the Great Controversy, volume four of the Spirit of Prophecy. It is printed in its entirety that nothing the author wrote has been omitted or changed. *"The Destruction of Jerusalem"* is the central focus of this study. It will show the reader sharp contrast between ancient and modern Jerusalem/ Israel (SDA). For easy reference, the original pagination is indicated at the end of the paragraph as <4SP>. Also, the "Introduction" by Ellen G. White to the 1884 edition of the Great Controversy is included. It deals with the plan of God in redeeming His remnant people during the final days of this earth's history.

"As He warned ***His disciples*** *of Jerusalem's destruction,* ***giving them a sign*** *of the approaching ruin that they might make their escape,* ***so He has warned His people*** *of the day of final destruction, and* ***given them signs*** *of its approach, that all who will may flee from the wrath to come." —4SP, p. 28 [1884]*

The popularly known 1911 edition of the Great Controversy worded it differently. Notice, "As He warned His disciples of Jerusalem's destruction, ***giving them a sign*** *of the approaching ruin, that they might make their escape;* ***so He has warned the world*** *of the day of final destruction and has* ***given them tokens*** *of its approach, that all who will may flee from the wrath to come." —Great Controversy, p. 38. [1911]*

Warning **the world**, quite obvious, is totally different from warning **His people.** Christ followers were the only people inside Jerusalem who recognized the **sign** given by Him—the planting of **Roman banner**. The rest of the Jews inside Jerusalem did not understand the meaning of the sign. Therefore; they suffered famine, hunger, slavery and even death. The 1884 edition said **"given them signs of its approach."** The 1911 edition said **"given them tokens of its approach."** The differences in words are very crucial in correct understanding of prophecy. Does Jesus Christ give tokens instead of signs to His people? *"And there shall be* ***signs*** *in the sun, and in the moon, and in the stars; and upon the earth distress of nations, with perplexity; the sea and the waves roaring; Men's hearts failing them for fear, and for looking after those things which are coming on the earth: for the powers of heaven shall be shaken." —Luke 21:25-26*

There are many deliberate changes in the 1911 edition of the Great Controversy from that of the original 1884 edition, which will not be discussed here. Try comparing it for yourself and you will be surprised. My personal observation is that; the 1911 edition is as to the NIV of the Bible and the 1884 edition is as to the KJV.

To give you an example of NIV Bible perversion try this: "Blessed are those ***who wash their robes*** *that they may have the right to the tree of life and may go through the gates into the city!" —Revelation 22:14 [NIV]*

"Blessed are they ***that do His commandments*** *that they may have right to the tree of life, and may enter in through the gates into the city."—Revelation 22:14 [KJV]*

In the NIV, you need not keep the commandments of God, just wash your robes and you go straight through the gates into the city. You can not even prove the Sanctuary doctrine using NIV.

The three different versions of the Great Controversy—1884, 1888, and 1911 had its purposes. These books are the most hated by Satan next to the Bible. As for me, I would prefer using the original 1884 G.C. version, and of course the 1611 King James Bible. You can request from Present Truth Global Ministries the 1884 original version of Great Controversy in MS Word form or the book itself.

"For I testify unto every man that heareth the words of the prophecy of this book, ***If any man shall add unto these things, God shall add unto him the plagues that are written in this book:*** *And if any man shall take away from the words of the book of this prophecy, God shall take away his part out of the book of life, and out of the holy city, and [from] the things which are written in this book."—Revelation 22:18-19*

"Blessed [is] he that readeth, *and they that* **hear** *the words of this prophecy, and* **keep** *those things which are written therein: for the* **time [is] at hand**.*"—Revelation 1:3*

All emphasize in bold letters, underlines, and some brackets throughout the chapters are mine. Bible and Spirit of Prophecy quotations are in italics. The Bible texts are from King James Version, unless otherwise indicated.

Compiler

INTRODUCTION TO THE GREAT CONTROVERSY

By Ellen G. White

Before the entrance of sin, Adam enjoyed open communion with his Maker; but since man separated himself from God by transgression, the human race has been cut off from this high privilege. By the plan of redemption, however, a way has been opened whereby the inhabitants of the earth may still have connection with heaven. God has communicated with men by His Spirit, and divine light has been imparted to the world by revelations to His chosen servants. "Holy men of God spake as they were moved by the Holy Ghost." 2 Peter 1:21 <GC v.1>

During the first twenty-five hundred years of human history, there was no written revelation. Those who had been taught of God, communicated their knowledge to others, and it was handed down from father to son, through successive generations. The preparation of the written word began in the time of Moses. Inspired revelations were then embodied in an inspired book. This work continued during the long period of sixteen hundred years—from Moses, the historian of creation and the law, to John, the recorder of the most sublime truths of the gospel. <GC v.2>

The Bible points to God as its author; yet it was written by human hands; and in the varied style of its different books it presents the characteristics of the several writers. The truths revealed are all "given by inspiration of God" (2 Timothy 3:16); yet they are expressed in the words of men. The Infinite One by His Holy Spirit has shed light into the minds and hearts of His servants. He has given dreams and visions, symbols and figures; and those to whom the truth was thus revealed have themselves embodied the thought in human language. <GC v.3>

The Ten Commandments were spoken by God Himself, and were written by His own hand. They are of divine, and not of human composition. But the Bible, with its God-given truths expressed in the language of men, presents a union of the divine and the human. Such a union existed in the nature of Christ, who was the Son of God and the Son of man. Thus it is true of the Bible, as it was of Christ, that "the Word was made flesh, and dwelt among us." John 1:14 <GC v.4>

Written in different ages, by men who differed widely in rank and occupation, and in mental and spiritual endowments, the books of the Bible present a wide contrast in style, as well as diversity in the nature of the subjects unfolded. Different forms of expression are employed by different writers; often the same truth is more strikingly presented by one than by another. And as several writers present a subject under varied aspects and relations, there may appear, to the superficial, careless, or prejudiced reader, to be discrepancy or contradiction, where the thoughtful, reverent student, with clearer insight, discerns the underlying harmony. <GC vi.1>

As presented through different individuals, the truth is brought out in its varied aspects. One writer is more strongly impressed with one phase of the subject; he grasps those points that harmonize with his experience or with his power of perception and appreciation. Another seizes upon a different phase; and each, under the guidance of the Holy Spirit, presents what is most forcibly impressed upon his own mind—a different aspect of the truth in each, but a perfect harmony through all. And the truths thus revealed unite to form a perfect whole, adapted to meet the wants of men in all the circumstances and experiences of life. <GC vi.2>

God has been pleased to communicate His truth to the world by human agencies, and He Himself, by His Holy Spirit, qualified men and enabled them to do this work. He guided the mind in the selection of what to speak and what to write. The treasure was entrusted to earthen vessels, yet it is, nonetheless, from Heaven. The testimony is conveyed through the imperfect expression of human language, yet it is the testimony of God; and the obedient, believing child of God beholds in it the glory of a divine power, full of grace and truth. <GC vi.3>

In His word, God has committed to men the knowledge necessary for salvation. The Holy Scriptures are to be accepted as an authoritative, infallible revelation of His will. They are the standard of character, the revealer of doctrines, and the test of experience. "Every scripture inspired of God is also profitable for teaching, for reproof, for correction, for instruction which is in righteousness; that the man of God may be complete, furnished completely unto every good work." 2 Timothy 3:16, 17, R.V. <GC vii.1>

Yet the fact that God has revealed His will to men through His word has not rendered needless the continued presence and guiding of the Holy Spirit. On the contrary, the Spirit was promised by our Saviour, to open the word to His servants, to illuminate and apply its teachings. And since it was the Spirit of God that inspired the Bible, it is impossible that the teaching of the Spirit should ever be contrary to that of the word. <GC vii.2>

The Spirit was not given—nor can it ever be bestowed—to supersede the Bible; for the Scriptures explicitly state that the word of God is the standard by which all teaching and experience must be tested. Says the apostle John, "Believe not every spirit, but try the spirits whether they are of God: because many false prophets are gone out into the world." 1 John 4:1 And Isaiah declares, "To the law and to the testimony: if they speak not according to this word, it is because there is no light in them." Isaiah 8:20 <GC vii.3>

Great reproach has been cast upon the work of the Holy Spirit by the errors of a class that, claiming its enlightenment, profess to have no further need of guidance from the word of God. They are governed by impressions which they regard as the voice of God in the soul. But the spirit that controls them is not the Spirit of God. This following of impressions, to the neglect of the Scriptures, can lead only to confusion, to deception and ruin. It serves only to further the designs of the evil one. Since the ministry of the Holy Spirit is of vital importance to the church of Christ, it is one of the devices of Satan, through the errors of extremists and fanatics, to cast contempt upon the work of the Spirit and cause the people of God to neglect this source of strength which our Lord Himself has provided. <GC vii.4>

In harmony with the word of God, His Spirit was to continue its work throughout the period of the gospel dispensation. During the ages while the Scriptures of both the Old and the New Testament were being given, the Holy Spirit did not cease to communicate light to individual minds, apart from the revelations to be embodied in the Sacred Canon. The Bible itself relates how, through the Holy Spirit, men received warning, reproof, counsel, and instruction, in matters in no way relating to the giving of the Scriptures. And mention is made of prophets in different ages, of whose utterances nothing is recorded. In like manner, after the close of the canon of the Scripture, the Holy Spirit was still to continue its work, to enlighten, warn, and comfort the children of God. <GC viii.1>

Jesus promised His disciples, "The Comforter which is the Holy Ghost, whom the Father will send in My name, He shall teach you all things, and bring all things to your remembrance, whatsoever I have said unto you." **"When He, the Spirit of truth, is come, He will guide you into all truth: . . . and He will show you things to come." John 14:26; 16:13.** Scripture plainly teaches that these promises, so far from being limited to apostolic days, extend to the church of Christ in all ages. The Saviour assures His followers, "I am with you alway, even unto the end of the world." Matthew 28:20. And Paul declares that the gifts and manifestations of the Spirit were set in the church "for the perfecting of the saints, for the work of the ministry, for the edifying of the body of Christ: till we all come in the unity of the faith, and of the knowledge of the Son of God, unto a perfect man, unto the measure of the stature of the fullness of Christ." Ephesians 4:12, 13 <GC viii.2>

For the believers at Ephesus the apostle prayed, "That the God of our Lord Jesus Christ, the Father of glory, may give unto you the *Spirit of wisdom and revelation* in the knowledge of Him: *the eyes of your understanding being enlightened;* that ye may know what is the hope of His calling, and . . . what is the *exceeding greatness* of His power to us ward who believe." Ephesians 1:17-19. The ministry of the divine Spirit in enlightening the understanding and opening to the mind the deep things of God's holy word, was the blessing which Paul thus besought for the Ephesian church. <GC ix.1>

After the wonderful manifestation of the Holy Spirit on the Day of Pentecost, Peter exhorted the people to repentance and baptism in the name of Christ, for the remission of their sins; and he said: "Ye shall receive the gift of the Holy Ghost. For the promise is unto you, and to your children, and to all that are afar off, even as many as the Lord our God shall call." Acts 2:38, 39 <GC ix.2>

In immediate connection with the scenes of the great day of God, the Lord by the prophet Joel has promised a special manifestation of His Spirit. Joel 2:28. This prophecy received a partial fulfillment in the outpouring of the Spirit on the Day of Pentecost; but it will reach its full accomplishment in the manifestation of divine grace which will attend the closing work of the gospel. <GC ix.3>

The great controversy between good and evil will increase in intensity to the very close of time. In all ages the wrath of Satan has been manifested against the church of Christ; and God has bestowed His grace and Spirit upon His people to strengthen them to stand against the power of the evil one. When the apostles of Christ were to bear His gospel to the world and to record it for all future ages, they were especially endowed with the enlightenment of the Spirit. But as the church approaches her final deliverance, Satan is to work with greater power. He comes down "having great wrath, because he knoweth that he hath but a short time." Revelation 12:12. He will work "with all power and signs and lying wonders." 2 Thessalonians 2:9. For six thousand years that mastermind that once was highest among the angels of God has been wholly bent to the work of deception and ruin. And all the depths of satanic skill and subtlety acquired, all the cruelty developed, during these struggles of the ages, will be brought to bear against God's people in the final conflict. And in this time of peril the followers of Christ are to bear to the world the warning of the Lord's Second Advent; and a people are to be prepared to stand before Him at His coming, "without spot, and blameless." 2 Peter 3:14. At this time the special endowment of divine grace and power is not less needful to the church than in apostolic days. <GC ix.4>

Through the illumination of the Holy Spirit, the scenes of the long-continued conflict between good and evil have been opened to the writer of these pages. From time to time I have been permitted to behold the working, in different ages, of the great controversy between Christ, the Prince of life, the Author of our salvation, and Satan, the prince of evil, the author of sin, the first transgressor of God's holy law. Satan's enmity against Christ has been manifested against His followers. The same hatred of the principles of God's law, the same policy of deception, by which error is made to appear as truth, by which human laws are substituted for the law of God, and men are led to worship the creature rather than the Creator, may be traced in all the history of the past. Satan's efforts to misrepresent the character of God, to cause men to cherish a false conception of the Creator, and thus to regard Him with fear and hate rather than with love; his endeavors to set aside the divine law, leading the people to think themselves free from its requirements; and his persecution of those who dare to resist his deceptions, have been steadfastly pursued in all ages. They may be traced in the history of patriarchs, prophets, and apostles, of martyrs and reformers. <GC x.1>

In the great final conflict, Satan will employ the same policy, manifest the same spirit, and work for the same end as in all preceding ages. **That which has been, will be, except that the coming struggle will be marked with a terrible intensity such as the world has never witnessed**. Satan's deceptions will be more subtle, his assaults more determined. If it were possible, he would lead astray the elect. Mark 13:22, R.V. <GC xi.1>

As the Spirit of God has opened to my mind the great truths of His word, and the scenes of the past and the future, I have been bidden to make known to others that which has thus been revealed—to trace the history of the controversy in past ages, and especially so to present it as to shed a light on the fast-approaching struggle of the future. In pursuance of this purpose, I have endeavored to select and group together events in the history of the church in such a manner as to trace the unfolding of the great testing truths that at different periods have been given to the world, that have excited the wrath of Satan, and the enmity of a world-loving church, and that have been maintained by the witness of those who "loved not their lives unto the death." <GC xi.2>

In these records we may see a foreshadowing of the conflict before us. Regarding them in the light of God's word, and by the illumination of His Spirit, we may see unveiled the devices of the wicked one, and the dangers which they must shun who would be found "without fault" before the Lord at His coming. <GC xi.3>

The great events which have marked the progress of reform in past ages are matters of history, well known and universally acknowledged by the Protestant world; they are facts which none can gainsay. This history I have presented briefly, in accordance with the scope of the book, and the brevity which must necessarily be observed, the facts having been condensed into as little space as seemed consistent with a proper understanding of their application. In some cases where a historian has so grouped together events as to afford, in brief, a comprehensive view of the subject, or has summarized details in a convenient manner, his words have been quoted; but in some instances no specific credit has been given, since the quotations are not given for the purpose of citing that writer as authority, but because his statement affords a ready and forcible presentation of the subject. In narrating the experience and views of those carrying forward the work of reform in our own time, similar use has been made of their published works. <GC xi.4>

It is not so much the object of this book to present new truths concerning the struggles of former times, as to bring out facts and principles which have a bearing on coming events. Yet viewed as a part of the controversy between the forces of light and darkness, all these records of the past are seen to have a new significance; and through them a light is cast upon the future, illumining the pathway of those who, like the reformers of past ages, will be called, even at the peril of all earthly good, to witness "for the word of God, and for the testimony of Jesus Christ." <GC xii.1>

To unfold the scenes of the great controversy between truth and error; to reveal the wiles of Satan, and the means by which he may be successfully resisted; to present a satisfactory solution of the great problem of evil, shedding such a light upon the origin and the final disposition of sin as to make fully manifest the justice and benevolence of God in all His dealings with His creatures; and to show the holy, unchanging nature of His law, is the object of this book. That through its influence souls may be delivered from the power of darkness, and become "partakers of the inheritance of the saints in light," to the praise of Him who loved us, and gave Himself for us, is the earnest prayer of the writer. ***—Ellen G. White***

CHAPTER 1

THE DESTRUCTION OF JERUSALEM (FROM VOLUME 4 OF THE SPIRIT OF PROPHECY WHICH IS THE 1884 EDITION OF THE GREAT CONTROVERSY, BY ELLEN G. WHITE)

"The days shall come upon thee, that thine enemies shall cast a trench about thee, and compass thee round, and keep thee in on every side, and shall lay thee even with the ground, and thy children within thee; and they shall not leave in thee one stone upon another; because thou knewest not the time of thy visitation." *[Luke 19:43, 44] <4SP 17.1>

From the crest of Olivet, Jesus looks upon Jerusalem. Fair and peaceful is the scene spread out before him. In the midst of gardens, vineyards, and green slopes studded with pilgrims' tents, rise the terraced hills, the stately palaces, and massive bulwarks of Israel's capital. The daughter of Zion seems in her pride to say, "I sit a queen, and shall see no sorrow;" as lovely now, and deeming herself as secure in Heaven's favor, as when, ages before, the royal minstrel sung, "Beautiful for situation, the joy of the whole earth, is Mount Zion," "the city of the great King." *[Ps. 48:2] In full view are the magnificent buildings of the temple. The rays of the setting sun light up the snowy whiteness of its marble walls, and gleam from golden gate and tower and pinnacle. "The perfection of beauty" it stands the pride of the Jewish nation. What child of Israel could gaze upon the scene without a thrill of joy and admiration! But far other thoughts occupy the mind of Jesus. "When He was come near, **He beheld the city, and wept over it."** *[Luke 19:41] Amid the universal rejoicing of the triumphal entry, while palm branches wave, while glad hosannas awake the echoes of the hills, and thousands of voices declare him king, the world's Redeemer is overwhelmed with a sudden and mysterious sorrow. He, the Son of God, the Promised One of Israel, whose power has conquered death, and called its captives from the grave, is in tears, not of ordinary grief, but of intense, irrepressible agony. <4SP 17.2>

His tears were not for Himself, though He well knew whither His feet were tending. Before Him lay Gethsemane. Not far distant was the place of crucifixion. Upon the path which He was soon to tread must fall the horror of great darkness as He should make His soul an offering for sin. Yet it was not a contemplation of these scenes that cast the shadow upon Him in this hour of gladness. No forebodings of His superhuman anguish clouded that unselfish spirit. He wept for the doomed thousands of Jerusalem,—because of the blindness and impenitence of those whom He came to bless and save. <4SP 18.1>

The history of a thousand years of privilege and blessing, granted to the Jewish people, was unfolded to the eye of Jesus. The Lord had made Zion His holy habitation. There prophets had unsealed their rolls and uttered their warnings. There priests had waved their censers, and daily offered the blood of slain lambs, pointing forward to the Lamb of God. There had Jehovah dwelt in visible glory, in the shekinah above the mercy-seat. There rested the base of that mystic ladder connecting earth with Heaven,—that ladder upon which angels of God descended and ascended, and which opened to the world the way into the holiest of all. Had Israel as a nation preserved her allegiance to Heaven, Jerusalem would have stood forever, the elect metropolis of God. But the history of that favored people was a record of backsliding and rebellion. They had resisted Heaven's grace, abused their privileges, and slighted their opportunities. <4SP 18.2>

Amid forgetfulness and apostasy, God had dealt with Israel as a loving father deals with a rebellious son, admonishing, warning, correcting, and still saying in the tender anguish of a parent's soul, how can I give thee up? When remonstrance, entreaty, and rebuke had failed, God sent to this people the best gift of Heaven; nay, he poured out to them all Heaven in that one gift. <4SP 19.1>

For three years, the Son of God knocked at the gate of the impenitent city. He came to His vineyard seeking fruit. Israel had been as a vine transplanted from Egypt into a genial soil. He dug about His vine; He pruned and cherished it. He was unwearied in His efforts to save this vine of His own planting. For three years, the Lord of light and glory had gone in and out among His people. He healed the sick; He comforted the sorrowing; he raised the dead; He spoke pardon and peace to the repentant. He gathered about Him the weak and the weary, the helpless and the desponding, and extended to all, without respect to age or character, the invitation of mercy: "Come unto me, all ye that labor and are heavy-laden and I will give you rest." *[Matt. 11:28] <4SP 19.2>

Regardless of indifference and contempt, He had steadfastly pursued His ministry of love. No frown upon His brow repelled the suppliant. Himself subjected to privation and reproach, He had lived to scatter blessings in His path, to plead with men to accept the gift of life. The waves of mercy, beaten back by the stubborn heart, returned in a tide of untiring love. But Israel had turned from her best friend and only helper. The pleadings of His love had been despised, His counsels spurned, His warnings ridiculed. <4SP 20.1>

The hour of grace and reprieve was fast passing; the cup of God's long-deferred wrath was almost full. The cloud of wrath that had been gathering through ages of apostasy and rebellion, was about to burst upon a guilty people, and He who alone could save them from their impending fate had been slighted, abused, rejected, and was soon to be crucified. When Christ should hang on Calvary's cross, Israel's day as a nation favored and blessed of God would be ended. The loss of even one soul is a calamity in comparison with which the gain of a world sinks into insignificance; but as Christ looked upon Jerusalem, the doom of a whole city, a whole nation, was before Him; that city, that nation which had once been the chosen of God,—His peculiar treasure. <4SP 20.2>

Prophets had wept over the apostasy of Israel. Jeremiah wished that his eyes were a fountain of tears that he might "weep day and night for the slain of the daughter of his people." What, then, was the grief of Him whose prophetic glance took in, not years, but ages? He beholds the destroying angel hovering over the ancient metropolis of patriarchs and prophets. From the ridge of Olivet, the very spot afterward occupied by Titus and his army, He looks across the valley upon the sacred courts and porticoes, and with tear-blinded eyes He sees, in awful perspective, the walls surrounded by alien armies. He hears the tread of the hosts mustering for battle. He hears the voice of mothers and children crying for bread in the besieged city. He sees her holy and beautiful house, her palaces and towers, given to the flames, and where once they stood, only a heap of smoldering ruins. <4SP 20.3>

He looks down the ages, and sees the covenant people scattered in every land, like wrecks on a dessert shore. He sees in the temporal retribution about to fall upon her children, but the first draught from that cup of wrath which at the final Judgment she must drain to its dregs. Divine pity, yearning love, finds utterance in the mournful words: "O Jerusalem, Jerusalem, thou that killest the prophets, and stonest them which are sent unto thee, how often would I have gathered thy children together, even as a hen gathereth her chickens under her wings, and ye would not!" *[Matt. 23.37] Oh that thou, a nation favored above every other, hadst known the time of thy visitation, and the things that belong unto thy peace! I have stayed the angel of justice; I have called thee to repentance, but all in vain. It is not merely servants, delegates, and prophets, whom thou hast refused and rejected, but the Holy One of Israel, thy Redeemer. If thou art destroyed, thou art alone responsible. "Ye will not come to me that ye might have life." <4SP 21.1>

Christ saw in Jerusalem a symbol of a world hardened in unbelief and rebellion, and rushing on to meet the retributive judgments of God. The woes of a fallen race, pressing upon his soul, forced from his lips that exceeding bitter cry. He saw the record of sin traced in human misery, in tears and blood; His heart was moved with infinite pity for the afflicted and suffering ones of earth; He yearned to relieve all. But He knew that even His hand might not turn back the incoming tide of human woe; few would seek their only source of help. He was willing to suffer and to die to bring salvation within their reach; but few would come to Him that they might have life. <4SP 22.1>

The Majesty of Heaven in tears! The Son of the infinite God troubled in spirit, bowed down with anguish! The scene filled all Heaven with wonder. That scene reveals to us the exceeding sinfulness of sin; it shows how hard a task it is, even for infinite power, to save the guilty from the consequences of transgressing the law of God. Jesus, looking down to the last generation, saw the world enclosed in a deception similar to that which caused the destruction of Jerusalem. **The great sin of the Jews was their rejection of Christ; the great sin of the Christian world would be their rejection of the law of God, the foundation of His government in Heaven and earth.** The precepts of Jehovah would be despised and set at naught. Millions in bondage to sin, slaves of Satan, doomed to suffer the second death, would refuse to listen to the words of truth in their day of visitation. Terrible blindness! Strange infatuation! <4SP 22.2>

Two days before the Passover, when Christ had for the last time departed from the temple, after denouncing the hypocrisy of the Jewish rulers, He again went out with His disciples to the Mount of Olives, and seated Himself with them upon a grassy slope overlooking the city. Once more He gazed upon its walls, its towers and palaces. Once more He beheld the temple in its dazzling splendor, a diadem of beauty crowning the sacred mount. <4SP 23.1>

A thousand years before had the psalmist magnified God's favor to Israel in making her holy house His dwelling place: "In Salem is His tabernacle, and His dwelling-place in Zion." *[Ps. 76:2] "He chose the tribe of Judah, the Mount Zion which He loved. And He built His sanctuary like high palaces." *[Ps. 78:68, 69] The first temple had been erected during the most prosperous period of Israel's history. Vast stores of treasure for this purpose had been collected by King David, and the plans for its construction were made by divine inspiration. **Solomon, the wisest of Israel's monarchs, had completed the work. This temple was the most magnificent building which the world ever saw. Yet the Lord had declared by**

the prophet Haggai, concerning the second temple, "The glory of this latter house shall be greater than of the former." "I will shake all nations, and the Desire of all nations shall come, and I will fill this house with glory, saith the Lord of hosts." *[Hag. 2:9, 7] <4SP 23.2>

After the destruction of the temple by Nebuchadnezzar, it was rebuilt about five hundred years before the birth of Christ, by a people who from a lifelong captivity had returned to a wasted and almost deserted country. There were then among them aged men who had seen the glory of Solomon's temple, and who wept at the foundation of the new building, that it must be so inferior to the former. The feeling that prevailed is forcibly described by the prophet: "Who is left among you that saw this house in her first glory? And how do ye see it now? Is it not in your eyes in comparison of it as nothing?" *[Hag. 2:3] Then was given the promise that the glory of this latter house should be greater than of the former. <4SP 23.3>

But the second temple had not equaled the first in magnificence; nor was it hallowed by those visible tokens of the divine presence which pertained to the first temple. There was no manifestation of supernatural power to mark its dedication. No cloud of glory was seen to fill the newly erected sanctuary. No fire from Heaven descended to consume the sacrifice upon its altar. The shekinah no longer abode between the cherubim in the most holy place; the ark, the mercy-seat, and the tables of the testimony were not to be found therein. No voice sounded from Heaven to make known to the inquiring priest the will of Jehovah. <4SP 24.1>

For centuries, the Jews had vainly endeavored to show wherein the promise of God, given by Haggai, had been fulfilled; yet pride and unbelief blinded their minds to the true meaning of the prophet's words. The second temple was not honored with the cloud of Jehovah's glory, but with the living presence of One in whom dwelt the fullness of the Godhead bodily,—who was God himself manifest in the flesh. The "Desire of all nations" had indeed come to his temple when the Man of Nazareth taught and healed in the sacred courts. In the presence of Christ, and in this only, did the second temple exceeds the first in glory. But Israel had put from her the proffered gift of Heaven. With the humble Teacher who had that day passed out from its golden gate, the glory had forever departed from the temple. Already were fulfilled the Saviour's words, "Your house is left unto you desolate." *[Matt. 23:38] <4SP 24.2>

The disciples had been filled with awe and wonder at Christ's prediction of the overthrow of the temple, and they desired to understand more fully the meaning of his words. Wealth, labor, and architectural skill had for more than forty years been freely expended to enhance its splendors. Herod the Great had lavished upon it both Roman wealth and Jewish treasure, and even the emperor of the world had enriched it with His gifts. Massive blocks of white marble, of almost fabulous size, forwarded from Rome for this purpose, formed a part of its structure; and to these the disciples had called the attention of their Master, saying, "See what manner of stones and what buildings are here!" *[Mark 13:1] <4SP 25.1>

To these words, Jesus made the solemn and starting reply, "Verily I say unto you, there shall not be left here one stone upon another that shall not be thrown down." *[Matt. 24:2] <4SP 25.2>

With the overthrow of Jerusalem the disciples associated the events of Christ's personal coming in temporal glory to take the throne of universal empire, to punish the impenitent Jews, and to break from off the nation the Roman yoke. The Lord had told them that he would come the second time. Hence at the mention of judgments upon Jerusalem, their minds revert to that coming, and as they are gathered about the Saviour upon the Mount of Olives, they ask, "When shall these things be? And what shall be the sign of thy coming, and of the end of the world?" *[Matt. 24:3] <4SP 25.3>

The future was mercifully veiled from the disciples. Had they at that time fully comprehended the two awful facts, — the Redeemer's sufferings and death and the destruction of their city and temple,—they would have been paralyzed with horror. Christ presented before them an outline of the prominent events to transpire before the close of time. His words were not then fully understood; but their meaning was to be unfolded as his people should need the instruction therein given. **The prophecy which He uttered was twofold in its meaning: while foreshadowing the destruction of Jerusalem, it prefigured also the terrors of the last great day. <4SP 26.1>**

Jesus declared to the listening disciples the judgments that were to fall upon apostate Israel and especially the retributive vengeance that would come upon them for their rejection and crucifixion of the Messiah. Unmistakable signs would precede the awful climax. The dreaded hour would come suddenly and swiftly. And the Saviour warned His followers: "When ye therefore shall see the abomination of desolation, spoken of by Daniel the prophet, stand in the holy place (whoso readeth let him understand), then let them which be in Judea flee into the mountains." *[Matt. 24:15, 16] When the idolatrous standards of the Romans should be set up in the holy ground, which extended some furlongs outside the city walls, then the followers of Christ were to find safety in flight. When the warning sign should be seen, judgment was to follow so quickly that those who would escape must make no delay. He who chanced to be upon the housetop must not go down through his house into the street; but he must speed his way from roof to roof until he reach the city wall, and be saved "so as by fire." Those who were working in the fields or vineyards must not take time to return for the outer garment laid aside while they should be toiling in the heat of the day. They must not hesitate a moment, lest they be involved in the general destruction. <4SP 26.2>

In the reign of Herod, Jerusalem had not only been greatly beautified, but by the erection of towers, walls, and fortresses, added to the natural strength of its situation, it had been rendered apparently impregnable. He who would at this time have foretold publicly its destruction, would, like Noah in his day, have been called a crazed alarmist. But Christ had said, "Heaven and earth shall pass away, but my words shall not pass away." *[Matt. 24:35] Because of her sins, wrath had been denounced against Jerusalem, and her stubborn unbelief rendered her doom certain. <4SP 27.1>

The Lord had declared by the prophet Micah: "Hear this, I pray you, ye heads of the house of Jacob, and princes of the house of Israel, that abhor judgment, and pervert all equity. They build up Zion with blood and Jerusalem with iniquity. The heads thereof judge for reward, and the priests thereof teach for hire, and the prophets thereof divine for money; yet will they lean upon the Lord, and say, is not the Lord among us? None evil can come upon us." *[Micah 3:9-11] <4SP 27.2>

How exactly did these words describe the corrupt and self-righteous inhabitants of Jerusalem! While claiming to rigidly observe the law of God, they were transgressing all its principles. They hated Christ because His purity and holiness revealed their iniquity; and they accused Him of being the cause of all the troubles which had come upon them in consequence of their sins. Though they knew Him to be sinless, they had declared that his death was necessary to their safety as a nation. "If we let Him thus alone," said the Jewish leaders, "all men will believe on Him; and the Romans shall come and take away both our place and nation." *[John 11:48] If Christ were sacrificed, they might once more become a strong, united people. Thus they reasoned, and they concurred in the decision of their high priest, that it would be better for one man to die than for the whole nation to perish. <4SP 28.1>

Thus had the Jewish leaders "built up Zion with blood and Jerusalem with iniquity." And yet, while they slew their Saviour because He reproved their sins, such was their self-righteousness that they regarded themselves as God's favored people, and expected the Lord to deliver them from their enemies. "Therefore," continued the prophet, "shall Zion for your sake be plowed as a field, and Jerusalem shall become heaps and the mountain of the house as the high places of the forest." *[Micah 3:12] <4SP 28.2>

For forty years after the doom of Jerusalem had been pronounced by Christ Himself, the Lord delayed His judgments upon the city and the nation. Wonderful was the long-suffering of God toward the rejecters of His gospel and the murderers of his Son. The parable of the unfruitful tree represented God's dealings with the Jewish nation. The command had gone forth. "Cut it down; why cumbereth it the ground?" *[Luke 13:7] But divine mercy had spared it yet a little longer. There were still many among the Jews who were ignorant of the character and the work of Christ. And the children had not enjoyed the opportunities or received the light which their parents had spurned. Through the preaching of the apostles and their associates, God would cause light to shine upon them; they could see how prophecy had been fulfilled, not only in the birth and life of Christ, but in His death and resurrection. The children were not condemned for the sins of the parents; but when, with knowledge of all the light given to their parents, the children rejected the additional light granted to themselves, they became partakers of the parents' sins, and filled up the measure of their iniquity. <4SP 28.3>

The long-suffering of God toward Jerusalem, only confirmed the Jews in their stubborn impenitence. In their hatred and cruelty toward the disciples of Jesus, they rejected the last offer of mercy. Then God withdrew His protection from them, and removed His restraining power from Satan and his angels, and the nation was left to the control of the leader she had chosen. Her children had spurned the grace of Christ, which would have enabled them to subdue their evil impulses, and now these became the conquerors. Satan aroused the fiercest and most debased passions of the soul. Men did not reason; they were beyond reason,—controlled by impulse and blind rage. They became Satanic in their cruelty. In the family and in the nation alike, among the highest and the lowest classes, there was suspicion, envy, hatred, strife, rebellion, murder. There was no safety anywhere. Friends and kindred betrayed one another. Parents slew their children and children their parents. The rulers of the people had no power to rule themselves. Uncontrolled passions made them tyrants. The Jews had accepted false testimony to condemn the innocent Son of God. Now false accusations made their own lives uncertain. By their actions they had long been saying, "Cause the Holy One of Israel to cease from before us." *[Isa. 30:11] Now their desire was granted. The fear of God no longer disturbed them. Satan was at the head of the nation and the highest civil and religious authorities were under his sway. <4SP 29.1>

The leaders of the opposing factions at times united to plunder and torture their wretched victims, and again they fell upon each other's forces, and slaughtered without mercy. Even the sanctity of the temple could not restrain their horrible ferocity. The worshipers were stricken down before the altar, and the sanctuary was polluted with the bodies of the slain. Yet in their blind and blasphemous presumption **the instigators of this hellish work publicly declared that they had no fear that Jerusalem would be destroyed, for it was God's own city**. To establish their power more firmly, they bribed false prophets to proclaim, even when Roman legions were besieging the temple that the people were to wait for deliverance from God. To the last, multitudes held fast to the belief that the Most High would interpose for the defeat of their adversaries. But Israel had spurned the divine protection, and now she had no defense. Unhappy Jerusalem! Rent by internal dissensions, the blood of her children, slain by one another's hands, crimsoning her streets, while alien armies beat down her fortifications and slew her men of war! <4SP 30.1>

All the predictions given by Christ concerning the destruction of Jerusalem were fulfilled to the letter. The Jews experienced the truth of his words of warning, "With what measure ye mete, it shall be measured to you again." <4SP 31.1>

Signs and wonders appeared, foreboding disaster and doom. A comet, resembling a flaming sword, for a year hung over the city. An unnatural light was seen hovering over the temple. Upon the clouds were pictured chariots mustering for battle. Mysterious voices in the temple court uttered the warning words, "Let us depart hence." The eastern gate of the inner court, which was of brass, and so heavy that it was with difficulty shut by a score of men, and having bolts fastened deep into the firm pavement, was seen at midnight to be opened of its own accord. <4SP 31.2>

For seven years, a man continued to go up and down the streets of Jerusalem, declaring the woes that were to come upon the city. By day and by night he chanted the wild dirge, "A voice from the east; a voice from the west; a voice from the four winds; a voice against Jerusalem and the temple; a voice against the bridegroom and the bride; and a voice against all the people." This strange being was imprisoned and scourged; but no complaint escaped his lips. To insult and abuse he answered only, "Woe to Jerusalem! Woe, woe to the inhabitants thereof!" His warning cry ceased not until he was slain in the siege he had foretold. <4SP 31.3>

Not one Christian perished in the destruction of Jerusalem. Christ had given His disciples warning and all who believed His words watched for the promised sign. After the Romans had surrounded the city, they unexpectedly withdrew their forces, at a time when everything seemed favorable for an immediate attack. In the providence of God the promised signal was thus given to the waiting Christians, and without a moment's delay they fled to a place of safety,—the refuge city Pella, in the land of Perea, beyond Jordan. <4SP 32.1>

Terrible were the calamities which fell upon Jerusalem in the siege of the city by Titus. The last desperate assault was made at the time of the Passover, when millions of Jews had assembled within its walls to celebrate the national festival. Their stores of provision, which if carefully preserved would have been sufficient to supply the inhabitants for years, had previously been destroyed through the jealousy and revenge of the contending factions, and now all the horrors of starvation were experienced. A measure of wheat was sold for a talent. Great numbers of the people would steal out at night, to appease their hunger by devouring herbs and wild plants growing outside the city walls, though they were often detected, and punished with torture and death. Some would gnaw the leather on their shields and sandals. The most inhuman tortures were inflicted by those in power to force from the want-stricken people the last scanty supplies which they might have concealed. And these cruelties were not infrequently practiced by men who were themselves well fed, and who were merely desirous of laying up a store of provision for the future. <4SP 32.2>

Thousands perished from famine and pestilence. Natural affection seemed to have been utterly destroyed. Children would be seen snatching the food from the mouths of their aged parents. The question of the prophet, "Can a woman forget her sucking child?" *[Isa. 49:15] Received the answer within the walls of that doomed city, "The hands of the pitiful women have sodden their own children; they were their meat in the destruction of the daughter of my people." *[Lam. 4:10] <4SP 33.1>

The Roman leaders endeavored to strike terror to the Jews, and thus cause them to surrender. Those prisoners, who resisted when taken, were scourged, tortured, and crucified before the wall of the city. Hundreds were daily put to death in this manner, and the dreadful work continued until, along the valley of Jehoshaphat and at Calvary, crosses were erected in so great numbers that there was scarcely room to move among them. So terribly was fulfilled the profane prayer uttered forty years before, "His blood be on us, and on our children." *[Matt. 27:25] <4SP 33.2>

Titus would willingly have put an end to the fearful scene, and thus have spared Jerusalem the full measure of her doom. He was filled with horror as he saw the bodies of the dead lying in heaps in the valleys. Like one entranced, he looked from the crest of Olivet upon the magnificent temple, and gave command that not one stone of it be touched. Before attempting to gain possession of this stronghold, he made an earnest appeal to the Jewish leaders not to force him to defile the sacred place with blood. If they would come forth and fight in any other place, no Roman should violate the sanctity of the temple. Josephus himself, in a most eloquent appeal, entreated them to surrender, to save themselves, their city, and their place of worship. But his words were answered with bitter curses. Darts were hurled at him, their last human mediator, as he stood pleading with them. The Jews had rejected the entreaties of the Son of God, and now expostulation and entreaty only made them more determined to resist to the last. In vain were the efforts of Titus to save the temple; One greater than he had declared that not one stone was to be left upon another. <4SP 33.3>

The blind obstinacy of the Jewish leaders, and the detestable crimes perpetrated within the besieged city, excited the horror and indignation of the Romans, and Titus at last decided to take the temple by storm. He determined, however, that if possible, it should be saved from destruction. But his commands were disregarded. After he had retired at night to his tent, the Jews, sallying from the temple, attacked the soldiers without. In the struggle, a firebrand was flung by a soldier through an opening in the porch, and immediately the chambers about the holy house were in a blaze. Titus rushed to the place, followed by his generals and legionaries, and commanded the soldiers to quench the flames. His words were unheeded. In their fury the soldiers hurled blazing brands into the chambers adjoining the temple, and then with their swords they slaughtered in great numbers those who had found shelter there. Blood flowed down the temple steps like water. Thousands upon thousands of Jews perished. Above the sound of battle were heard voices shouting, "Ichabod!"—the glory is departed. <4SP 34.1>

The fire had not reached the holy house itself when Titus entered, and, beholding its unsurpassed splendor, he was impelled to a last effort for its preservation. But in his very presence, a soldier thrust a lighted torch between the hinges of the door, and in an instant the flames burst out within the sanctuary. As the red glare revealed the walls of the holy places, glittering with gold, frenzy seized the soldiers. Goaded on by a desire for plunder, and filled with rage by the resistance of the Jews, they were beyond control. <4SP 35.1>

The lofty and massive structures that had crowned Mount Moriah were in flames. The temple towers sent up columns of fire and smoke. As the lurid tide rolled on, devouring everything before it, the whole summit of the hill blazed like a volcano. Mingled with the roar of the fire, the shouts of the soldiers, and the crash of falling buildings, were heard the frantic, heart-rending cries of old and young, priests and rulers. The very mountains seemed to give back the echo. The awful glare of the conflagration lighted up the surrounding country, and the people gathered upon the hills, and gazed in terror upon the scene. <4SP 35.2>

After the destruction of the temple, the whole city soon fell into the hands of the Romans. The leaders of the Jews forsook their impregnable towers, and Titus found them solitary. He gazed upon them with amazement, and declared that God had given them into his hands; for no engines, however powerful, could have prevailed against those stupendous battlements. Both the city and the temple were razed to their foundations, and the ground upon which the holy house had stood was "plowed as a field." More than a million of the people were slaughtered; the survivors were carried away as captives, sold as slaves, dragged to Rome to grace the conqueror's triumph, thrown to wild beasts in the amphitheaters, or scattered as homeless wanderers throughout the earth. <4SP 36.1>

The Jews had forged their own fetters; they had loaded for themselves the cloud of vengeance. In the utter destruction that befell them as a nation, and in all the woes that followed them in their dispersion, they were but reaping the harvest which their own hands had sown. Their sufferings are often represented as a punishment visited upon them by the direct decree of God. This is a device by which the great deceiver seeks to conceal his own work. By stubborn rejection of divine love and mercy, the Jews had caused the protection of God to be withdrawn from them, and Satan was permitted to rule them according to his will. The horrible cruelties enacted in the destruction of Jerusalem are a demonstration of Satan's vindictive power over those who yield to his control. <4SP 36.2>

We cannot know how much we owe to Christ for the peace and protection which we enjoy. It is the restraining power of God that prevents mankind from passing fully under the control of Satan. The disobedient and unthankful have great reason for gratitude for God's mercy and long-suffering in holding in check the cruel, malignant power of the evil one. But when men pass the limits of divine forbearance, that restraint is removed. God does not stand toward the sinner as an executioner of the sentence against transgression; but he leaves the rejecters of his mercy to themselves, to reap that which they have sown. Every ray of light rejected, every warning despised or unheeded, every passion indulged, every transgression of the law of God, is a seed sown, which yields its unfailing harvest. The Spirit of God, persistently resisted, is at last withdrawn from the sinner, and then there is left no power to control the evil passions of the soul, and no protection from the malice and enmity of Satan. The destruction of Jerusalem is a fearful and solemn warning to all who are trifling with the offers of divine grace, and turning away the pleadings of divine mercy. Never was given a more decisive testimony to God's hatred of sin, and to the certain punishment that will fall upon the guilty. <4SP 36.3>

The Saviour's prophecy concerning the visitation of judgments upon Jerusalem is to have another fulfillment, of which that terrible scene was but a faint shadow. The second advent of the Son of God is foretold by lips which make no mistake: "Then shall all the tribes of the earth mourn, and they shall see the Son of man coming in the clouds of heaven, with power and great glory. And He shall send his angels with a great sound of a trumpet, and they shall gather together His elect from the four winds, from one end of heaven to the other." *[Matt. 24:30, 31] Then shall they that obey not the gospel be consumed with the spirit of his mouth, and destroyed with the brightness of His coming. *[2 Thess. 2:8] <4SP 37.1>

Let men beware lest they neglect the lesson conveyed to them in the words of Christ. He has declared that He will come the second time, to gather His faithful ones to Himself, and to take vengeance on them that reject His mercy. **As He warned His disciples of Jerusalem's destruction, giving them a sign of the approaching ruin that they might make their escape, so He has warned His**

people of the day of final destruction, and given them signs of its approach, that all who will may flee from the wrath to come. Those who behold the promised signs are to "know that it is near, even at the door." "Watch ye therefore," are his words of admonition. "If thou shalt not watch, I will come on thee as a thief." <4SP 38.1>

The world is no more ready now to credit the warning than were the Jews in the days of our Saviour. Come when it may, the end will come unawares to the ungodly. When life is going on in its unvarying round; when men are absorbed in pleasure, in business, in traffic, in money-making; when religious leaders are magnifying the world's progress and enlightenment, and the people are lulled in a false security,—then, as the midnight thief steals within the unguarded dwelling, so shall sudden destruction come upon the careless and ungodly, "and they shall not escape." <4SP 38.2>

Destruction of Jerusalem by Titus in 70 A.D.

Inner relief of the Arch of Titus commemorates the destruction of Jerusalem. The seven-branched candlestick—the Menorah—and other items from the temple are paraded by the triumphant Romans as booty.

CHAPTER 2

JESUS CHRIST PROPHECY MATTHEW 24:15-22

Warning! (Sign to flee when the Roman banner is planted in Jerusalem)

> *When ye therefore shall see the abomination of desolation spoken of by Daniel the prophet, stand in the holy place, (whoso readeth, let him understand:)*

Sense of urgency to take action

> *Then let them which be in Judea flee into the mountains: Let him which is on the housetop not come down to take any thing out of his house: Neither let him which is in the field return back to take his clothes.*

Hardship for God's people

> *And woe unto them that are with child and to them that give suck in those days! But pray ye that your flight be not in the winter, neither on the Sabbath day:*

Great Tribulation such as was not

> *For then shall be great tribulation, such as was not since the beginning of the world to this time, no, nor ever shall be.*

Time is short

> *And except those days should be shortened, there should no flesh be saved: but for the elect's sake those days shall be shortened.*

Solemn Warning to Modern Jerusalem [SDA]

"The desolation in the days of Jeremiah is a solemn warning to ***modern Jerusalem.****"—Prophets and Kings, p. 417*

"Neglect to repent and obey His Word, will bring as serious consequences upon God's people today as did ancient Israel. *There is a limit beyond which He will no longer delay His judgments. The desolation of Jerusalem stands as a solemn warning before the eyes of* ***modern Israel****, that the corrections given through His chosen* *instruments cannot be disregarded with impunity."—4 Testimonies, p. 167*

"All the great events and solemn transactions of Old Testament history have been, and are, repeating themselves in the church in these last days."—3 Selected Messages, p. 339.

From the Spirit of Prophecy quotations above, notice the term modern Israel and modern Jerusalem in context, they are applicable to the Seventh-day Adventist church. The term modern Israel and modern Jerusalem is also synonymous to spiritual Israel, the chosen people of God in these last days.

"In a special sense ***Seventh-day Adventists have been set in the world as watchmen and light bearers.*** *To them has been entrusted the last warning for a perishing world. On them is shining wonderful light from the Word of God.* ***They have been given a work of the most solemn import—the proclamation of the first, second, and third angels' messages.*** *There is no other work of so great importance. They are to allow nothing else to absorb their attention."—9 Testimonies, p. 19. (1909).*

It is a very disturbing thought, however, that the destruction of ancient Jerusalem will be repeated to modern Jerusalem [SDA]. Spiritual destruction followed by physical. ***"The prophecy which He [Jesus] uttered was twofold in its meaning: while foreshadowing the destruction of Jerusalem, it prefigured also the terrors of the last great day."—4SP, p. 26***

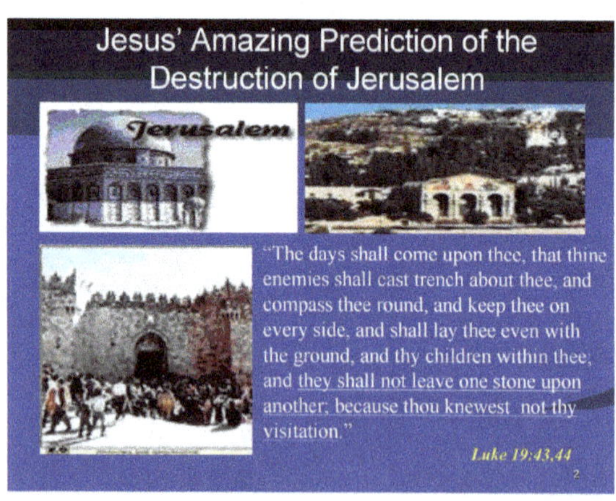

"The disciples had been filled with awe and wonder at Christ's prediction of the overthrow of the temple, and they desired to understand more fully the meaning of his words. "To these words, Jesus made the solemn and startling reply "Verily I say unto you, ***There shall not be left here one stone upon another, that shall not be thrown down."*** *— Matt. 24:2*

"All the predictions given by Christ concerning the destruction of Jerusalem were fulfilled to the letter."— 4SP, p. 31

This prophecy was fulfilled to the very letter in 70 A.D. during the siege of Roman General Titus in Jerusalem. When the temple at Jerusalem was burned and razed to the ground, the gold that was inlaid heavily in its curtains melted down and flowed into the crevices. Every stone was turned upside down "plowed as a field" to retrieve the gold. If you have read the book "Josephus" describing the carnage, cannibalism, famine, factionalism and lawlessness, the horrible destruction of Jerusalem will melt your flesh away from the very bones.

"The Saviour's prophecy concerning the visitation of judgments upon Jerusalem is to have another fulfillment, of which that terrible scene was but a faint shadow."— 4SP, p. 37

While the Bible prophecy concerning physical Israel is still valid, yet it has a direct application to spiritual Israel [SDA]. We can no longer keep our eyes closed to those prophecies because there are terrible consequences. **To be forewarned is to be forearmed.** If the judgment and destruction that befell upon ancient Jerusalem was just but a faint shadow, then what would it become of modern Jerusalem [SDA]? It behooves us to diligently study and pay attention to the warnings contained in the Word of God and the Spirit of Prophecy through the inspired writings of Mrs. Ellen G. White.

"Mark this point with care: Those who receive the pure mark of truth, wrought in them by the power of the Holy Ghost, represented by a mark by the man in linen, are those ***"that sigh and that cry for all the abominations that be done" in the church****. Their love for purity and the honor*

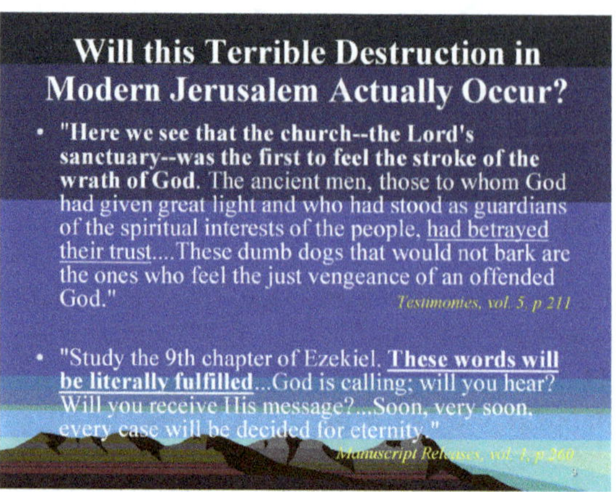

and glory of God is such, and they have so clear a view of the exceeding sinfulness of sin, that they are represented as being in agony, even sighing and crying. Read the ninth chapter of Ezekiel.

"But the general slaughter of all those who do not thus see the wide contrast between sin and righteousness, and do not feel as those who do stand in the counsel of God and receive the mark, is described in the order to the five men with slaughter weapons: 'Go ye after him through the city, and smite: let not your eye spare, neither have ye pity: slay utterly old and young, both maids, and little children, and women: but come not near any man upon whom is the mark; and begin at My sanctuary."—3 Testimonies, p. 267

"The Seal of God will be placed upon the foreheads of those only who sigh and cry for the abominations done in the church."—5 Testimonies, p. 212

*"At the time when the danger and depression of the church are greatest, **the little company who are standing in the light will be sighing and crying for the abominations that are done in the land.** But more especially will their prayers arise in behalf of the church because its members are doing after the manner of the world."—5 Testimonies, pp. 209-210*

The little company here mentioned is the Philadelphian SDA. They, who have chosen to adhere and remain faithful in the old Adventist historic theology that the pioneers have started. They follow the Lamb—Jesus, whithersoever He goeth. They have decided to not follow after the world. *"God has said: "Thou shalt not follow a multitude to do evil."—4T 647*

We can no longer afford to remain complacent. We should sigh and cry for all the abominations that has happened or is happening in the Seventh-day Adventist churches: introduction of New Theology; Celebration type of worship; Neuro-Linguistic Programming or hypnotism; jewelry wearing; investing tithes and offerings in stocks and bonds; trade marking the name "Seventh-day Adventist" and suing historic SDA in court; worldly accreditation of universities and colleges; joining the ecumenical World Council of Churches and National Council of Churches; having a United Nations liaison office inside the General Conference; and kindred strange theories and doctrines that had "crept" into the church. We can no longer remain neutral and indifferent to issues affecting the church.

"If God abhors one sin above another, of which His people are guilty, it is doing nothing in case of an emergency. Indifference and neutrality in a religious crisis is regarded of God as a grievous crime and equal to the very worst type of hostility against God."—3T 280 Where do you stand?

The Lord said, *"Cry aloud, spare not, lift up thy voice like a trumpet, and show my people their transgression, and the house of Jacob their sins." Isaiah 58:1.* We must be established in the "present truth," Early Writings, p. 63. [2 Peter 1:12], and purify our souls through faith and obedience to the commandments of God and Spirit of Prophecy.

"Just as soon as the people of God are sealed in their foreheads—it is not any seal or mark that can be seen, but a settling into the truth, both intellectually and spiritually, so they cannot be moved—just as soon as God's people are sealed and prepared for the shaking, it will come. Indeed, it has begun already."—4 SDA Bible Commentary, p. 116

Watch For the Sign That You May Escape

"Not one Christian perished in the destruction of Jerusalem. Christ had given His disciples warning and all

who believed His words watched for the promised sign. After the Romans had surrounded the city, they unexpectedly withdrew their forces, at a time when everything seemed favorable for an immediate attack. In the providence of God the promised signal was thus given to the waiting Christians, and without a moment's delay they fled to a place of safety,—the refuge city Pella, in the land of Perea, beyond Jordan." — 4SP, p. 32

"Jesus declared to the listening disciples the judgments that were to fall upon apostate Israel and especially the retributive vengeance that would come upon them for their rejection and crucifixion of the Messiah. Unmistakable signs would precede the awful climax. The dreaded hour would come ***suddenly and swiftly****. And the Saviour warned His followers:* ***"When ye therefore shall see the abomination of desolation, spoken of by Daniel the prophet, stand in the holy place (whoso readeth let him understand), then let them which be in Judea flee into the mountains."*** *[Matt. 24:15, 16] When the idolatrous standards of the Romans should be set up in the holy ground, which extended some furlongs outside the city walls, then the followers of Christ were to find safety in flight. When the warning sign should be seen, judgment was to follow so quickly that those who would escape must make no delay. He who chanced to be upon the housetop must not go down through his house into the street; but he must speed his way from roof to roof until he reach the city wall, and be saved "so as by fire." Those who were working in the fields or vineyards must not take time to return for the outer garment laid aside while they should be toiling in the heat of the day. They must not hesitate a moment, lest they be involved in the general destruction." —Great Controversy, p. 24-25*

There is a sense of urgency to the warning **"flee to the mountains."** Although the destruction of Jerusalem did not happen until 70 A.D. under General Titus, the followers of Christ called Christians were instructed to speed their way from roof to roof, and make no delay to escape "so as by fire."

According to Flavius Josephus, a Jewish historian, it was on Sabbath, October, 66 A.D. that the Jews were gathered in Jerusalem to celebrate the feast of Tabernacle, a holy convocation to them. Cestius Gallus, then governor of Syria, with his Roman legions marched toward Jerusalem for an invasion. Outside the walls of Jerusalem, there was an area considered as holy ground. On that particular place, he planted the Roman banner and for some reason immediately withdrew. As the Jewish troops clashed with the Roman soldiers, in the providence of God, the faithful Christians who watched for the promised sign were able to flee to the Judean Mountain.

What is the parallelism to modern Jerusalem [SDA]? We should really pray hard for spiritual discernment in order for us to understand the prophecy. "*When ye therefore shall see the abomination of desolation, spoken of by Daniel the prophet, stand in the holy place (whoso readeth let him understand).*"

It was customary for an attacking army in those days to lift their standard as a threatening sign of their power and intended overthrow. This action constituted the "Abomination of desolation standing in the holy place." In 1995 A.D. for the first time in the history of the Seventh-day Adventist church, the modern Roman banner—Vatican flag was planted in modern Jerusalem [SDA] at the General Conference session in Utrecht, Netherlands. The grand gathering every five years was considered to be a spiritual feast, a holy convocation for all Seventh-day Adventists present.

"He [Satan] has deceived them, benumbed their sensibilities, and planted his hellish banner right in their midst, and they are so completely deceived that they know not that it is he."—2 Testimonies, p. 440

The final siege for modern Jerusalem is when the final National Sunday law decree will be implemented in America and internationally. At that time, the Papal New World Order is in operation. No one will be able to buy or sell save he that has the mark of the beast. Study very carefully the "Sixteen Articles" presented by Pope John Paul II in Kenya, Africa, found in chapter 8 of this book.

Faithful Seventh-day Adventists will be cut-off from all earthly support. Hence, they will face hardship if they do not prepare a place in the country where they can plant their own food. Now is the time to prepare before it's too late! Ask for our studies in power point "The New World Order! A Prelude to the Second Coming of Jesus Christ as prophesied in the Bible, Revelation chapter 17. Also, you can request studies in "Country Living" and other interesting and important subjects.

Our total dependence will be upon God, not on the system. His grace will be sufficient for us. We are now living in the Day of Atonement when we have to afflict our souls before God, confess our sins to Him and develop a Christ-like character. We have to give the three angels' messages to the world. Jesus is coming soon! Are you ready?

"Christ is waiting with longing desire for the manifestation of Himself in His church. ***When the character of Christ shall be perfectly reproduced in His people, then He will come to claim them as His own."****—Christ Object Lesson, p. 69*

CHAPTER 3

WHO IS MODERN JERUSALEM?

"Jerusalem is a representation of what the church will be if it refuses to walk in the light that God has given. *Jerusalem was favored of God as the depository of sacred trusts. But her people perverted the truth, and despised all entreaties and warnings. They would not respect His counsels. The temple courts were polluted with merchandise and robbery. Selfishness and love of mammon, envy and strife, were cherished."—Special Testimonies Series B, pp. 48-49*

"I tell you all this that you may be enlightened, and may enlighten others, in regard to the character of the work in these missions. It is very difficult for those far distant to lift their eyes to see far off. They desire to build as they have done in Battle Creek, they will do so, adding building to building, when God has cautioned them not to do it. Battle Creek will not escape the dragon's wrath; there will be stormy times, perilous times. ***The interest that have centered and accumulating in this modern Jerusalem will be a mark for the arrows of Satan."****—Paulson Collection, p. 136*

At that time, the General Conference of Seventh-day Adventist headquarters, Battle Creek College and Battle Creek Sanitarium were all located in Battle Creek, Michigan, which was called **modern Jerusalem**. It was not in God's order that the work will be centralized in one place.

Destructions in Modern Jerusalem

"Today I received a letter from Elder Daniells, [General Conference president] regarding the destruction of the Review office by fire. I feel very sad as I consider the great loss to the cause. I know that this must be a very trying time for the brethren in charge of the work and for the employees of the office. I am afflicted with all who are afflicted. But I was not surprised by the sad news, for in the visions of the night I have seen an angel standing with a sword as of fire stretched over Battle Creek. Once, in the daytime while my

Review and Herald Publishing Association, Battle Creek, Michigan, taken before the fire which destroyed this building on December 30, 1902. Inset: J. H. Kellogg.

pen was in my hand, I lost consciousness, and it seemed as if this sword of flame were turning first in one direction and then in another. Disaster seemed to follow disaster [SEVENTH-DAY ADVENTIST FIRES IN BATTLE CREEK DESTROYED NOT ONLY THE SANITARIUM BUILDING AND THE REVIEW AND HERALD FACTORY BUT ALSO THE HASKELL ORPHAN HOME. AND THERE WERE OTHER FIRES OF LESS CONSEQUENCE. NO MORE CONVINCING DISAPPROVAL OF THE STATUS QUO COULD HAVE BEEN PROVIDED BY THE MASTER OVERSEER OF THE WORK THAN THESE CALAMITIES] because God was dishonored by the devising of men to exalt and glorify themselves."— Publishing Ministry, p. 172

"Satan's chief work is at the headquarters of our faith. *He spares no pain to corrupt men in responsible positions and to persuade them to be unfaithful to their several trusts. It is Satan's plan to weaken the faith of God's people in Testimonies. Next follows skepticism in regard to the vital points of our faith, the pillars of our position, then doubt as to the Holy Scriptures, and then downward march to perdition. When the Testimonies, which were once believed, are doubted and given up, Satan knows the deceived once will not stop at this; and he redoubles his efforts till he launches them into open rebellion, which*

becomes incurable and ends in destruction."—Testimonies, vol. 4, pp. 210-211

"The headquarters of our church, affect the whole body of believers. *If the physical heart is healthy, the blood that is sent from it through the system is also healthy; but if this fountain is impure, the organism becomes diseased by the poison of the vital fluid. So it is with us. If the heart of the work becomes corrupt, the whole church, in its various branches and interest, scattered abroad over the face of the earth, suffers in consequence."—4 Testimonies, p. 210*

"The sin of ***ancient Israel*** *was in disregarding the expressed will of God and following in their own way according to the leadings of unsanctified hearts.* ***Modern Israel (SDA)*** *is fast following in their steps, and the displeasure of the Lord is as surely resting upon them."—5 Testimonies, p. 94*

Ancient Israel and Modern Israel [SDA] Contrasted

"Like ancient Israel, the church (SDA) has dishonored her God by departing from the light, *neglecting her duties, and abusing her high exalted privilege of being peculiar and holy in character. Her members have violated their covenant to live for God and Him only. They have joined* *the selfish and world loving. Pride, the love of pleasure and sin has been cherished, and* ***Christ has departed. His Spirit (Spirit of Prophecy) has been quenched in the church."***—*2 Testimonies, p. 441-442*

Same Sin Have Delayed Entrance of Modern Israel [SDA]

"It was not the will of God that the coming of Christ should be thus delayed. God did not design that His people, Israel, should wander forty years in the wilderness. He promised to lead them directly to the land of Canaan, and establish them there a holy, healthy, happy people. But those, to whom it was first preached, went not in ***"because of unbelief."*** *Their hearts were filled with murmuring, rebellion, and hatred and He could not fulfill His covenant with them.*

"For forty years did unbelief, murmuring, and rebellion ***shut out ancient Israel from the land of Canaan****. The same sins have* ***delayed the entrance of modern Israel into the heavenly Canaan.*** *In neither case were the promises of God at fault. It is the unbelief, the worldliness, unconsecration, and strife among the Lord's professed people that have kept us in this world of sin and sorrow so many years."—Manuscript 4, 1883; Evangelism, p. 696*

CHAPTER 4

WARNING TO MODERN JERUSALEM!

"As He warned His disciples of Jerusalem's destruction, giving them a sign of the approaching ruin that they might make their escape, ***so He has warned His people of the day of final destruction, and given them signs of its approach, that all who will may flee from the wrath to come.*** *Those who behold the promised signs are to "know that it is near, even at the door." "Watch ye therefore," are his words of admonition. "If thou shalt not watch, I will come on thee as a thief."* <4SP 38.1>

For the first time in the history of modern Jerusalem (SDA) at the 1995 General Conference of Seventh-day Adventist in Utrecht, Netherlands, the Vatican flag was paraded and most applauded during the "Parade of Nations." This colorful but solemn event marks the culmination of the General Conference session. Each flag represents a country which has Seventh-day Adventist church or believers. It is a known fact that there is not a single Seventh-day Adventist inside the Vatican City—

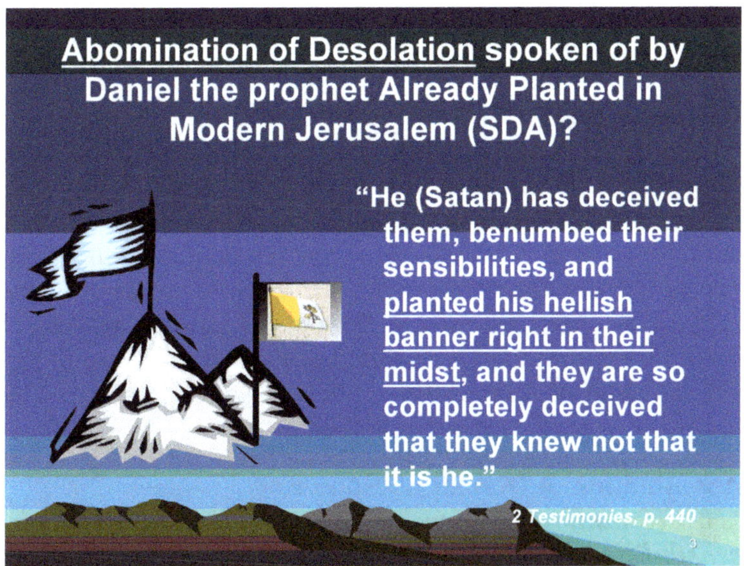

a State within a State. People who reside there are the Priests, Nuns, Cardinals, the Pope, and their employees. In the Archives and Statistics of General Conference of SDA, Vatican City was listed as un-entered; population—1,000; churches—0; members—0. I could see no valid reason why the Vatican flag should be there in the first place. Could this be the fulfillment of the prophecy concerning modern Jerusalem [SDA], the final warning before destruction?

"And the Saviour warned His followers: "When ye therefore shall see the abomination of desolation, spoken of by Daniel the prophet, stand in the holy place (whoso readeth let him understand), then let them which be in Judea flee into the mountains." [Matt. 24:15, 16.] When the idolatrous standards of the Romans should be set up in the holy ground, which extended some furlongs outside the city walls, then the followers of Christ were to find safety in flight."—Great Controversy, p. 24-25

Abomination of Desolation Stands

"He [Satan] has deceived them, benumbed their sensibilities, and planted his hellish banner right in their

midst, and they are so completely deceived that they know not that it is he."—2 Testimonies, p. 440

"One thing is certain: Those Seventh-day Adventists who take their stand under Satan's banner will first give up their faith in the warnings and reproofs contained in the Testimonies of God's Spirit."—3 Selected Messages, p. 48

"Men may get up scheme after scheme, and the enemy will seek to seduce souls from the Truth but all who believe that the Lord has spoken through Sister White and has given her a message, will be safe from the many delusions that will come in these last days."—3 SM, p. 83-84.

"Those who behold the promised signs are to "know that it is near, even at the door." "Watch ye therefore," are His words of admonition. "If thou shalt not watch, I will come on thee as a thief."—4SP, p. 38.

Significance of Planting the Banner

The planting of the American flag in that small island of Japan called Iwo Jima by the U.S. troops during World War II was a sign of their conquest of the territory. When U.S. astronauts Neil Armstrong and Buzz Aldrin first landed on the Moon in 1969, they first planted the American flag, which was a symbol of their conquest of the lunar territory.

Jesus Christ prophecy is to have another fulfillment, this time in modern Jerusalem [SDA]. In 1995, at the General Conference session at Utrecht, Netherlands, when all the Seventh-day Adventist representatives from all over the world were gathered during a holy convocation, the modern Roman banner—the Vatican flag, the abomination of desolation spoken of by Daniel the prophet was planted. ***"Thine enemies roar in the midst of thy congregation; they***

set up their ensigns [for] signs."—Psalms 74:4. Who were able to discern it? Instead of fleeing, as the flag was being waved back and forth as to a racing car reaching the finish line, you could hear the thundering applause from the congregation. Had the Vatican—the woman of Revelation 17 conquered the territory?

"When ye therefore shall see the abomination of desolation, spoken of by Daniel the prophet, stand in the holy place (whoso readeth let him understand), then let them which be in Judea flee into the mountains."—Matt.24:15, 16

"Not one Christian perished in the destruction of Jerusalem. Christ had given His disciples warning, and all who <u>believed</u> His words <u>watched</u> for the promised sign."—4SP, p. 32

Out of the Cities

"Who will be warned? We say again, Out of the cities. Do not consider it a great deprivation that you must go into the hills and mountains, but seek for that retirement where you can be alone with God, to learn His will and way...I urge our people to make it their lifework to seek for spirituality. ***Christ is at the door. This is why I say to our people. Do not consider it a privation when you are called to leave the cities and move into the country places****. Here await rich blessings for those who will grasp them. By beholding the scenes of nature, the works of the Creator, by studying God's handiwork, imperceptibly you will be changed into the same image."—(MS 85, 1908). Also, 2 Selected Messages, p. 355,356*

"We see efforts are being made to restrict our religious liberty. The Sunday question is now assuming large proportions. An amendment to our constitution is being urged in Congress, AND WHEN IT IS OBTAINED, OPPRESSION MUST FOLLOW."—RH Dec 18, 1888

"Here's one my conservative base is REALLY going to like. A constitutional amendment requiring folks to attended church on Sundays!"—Pres. George Bush, Jr. An Editorial Cartoon that appeared in February 26, 2004, Daytona Beach News Journal. Is he showing us a tell tale sign?

When National Sunday law is declared in America, and becomes an International Sunday law for the whole world, the only safe place during the time of trouble will be the one that is designated by God as city of refuge—**hills and mountains or Country Living.** We are admonished by the Lord to go to a country place where we could purchase a piece of land and plant our own produce. Time will come when the issue of buying and selling will be a very serious one, and if you don't have the mark, the name of the beast, or the number of his name, you will not be able to transact business with them.

Mark of the Beast Explained

There are three elements mentioned: the mark which is Sunday worship when it becomes a law; the name of the beast which is vicarious filii dei; or the number of his name which is 666.

"Sunday keeping is not yet the mark of the beast and will not be until the (Sunday Law) DECREE goes forth causing men to worship this idol sabbath. ***The time will come when this day will be the test*** *but the time has not yet come."—7 BC 977.*

Preparation for Country Living

"The Lord desires His people to move into the country, where they can settle on the land, and raise their own fruit and vegetables, and where their children can be brought in direct contact with the works of God in nature. ***Take your families away from the cities, is my message."****—2SM, p. 357-358*

"The physical surroundings in the cities are often a peril to health. The constant liability to contact with disease, the prevalence of foul air, impure water, impure food, the crowded, dark, unhealthful dwellings, are some of the many evils to be met. It was not God's purpose that people should be crowded into cities, huddled together in terraces and tenements."—Ministry of Healing, p. 365

Study the booklet entitled "Country Living" by Ellen G. White. It will help you in making a decision whether for life or for death. Inspiration says that in the last days ***"God's people will be cut-off from all earthly support."*** At that time, our loving **God will extend to us His heavenly support.**

Troublous Times Before Us

"We are not to locate ourselves where we will be forced into close relations with those who do not honor God. . . . A crisis is soon to come in regard to the observance of Sunday. The Sunday party is strengthening itself in its false claims, and this will mean oppression to those who determine to keep the Sabbath of the Lord. We are to place ourselves where we can carry out the Sabbath commandment in its fullness. "Six days shalt thou labor," the Lord declares, "and do all thy work; but the seventh day is the Sabbath of the Lord thy God: in it thou shalt not do any work." And we are to be careful not to place ourselves where it will be hard for ourselves and our children to keep the Sabbath."—Country Living, p. 20

"Instead of spending our means in self-gratification, we should be studying to economize. Every talent lent of God should be used to His glory in giving the warning to the world. God has a work for His co-laborers to do in the cities. Our missions must be sustained; new missions must be opened. To carry forward this work successfully will require no small outlay. Houses of worship are needed, where the

people may be invited to hear the truths for this time. For this very purpose, God has entrusted a capital to His stewards. Let not your property be tied up in worldly enterprises, so that this work shall be hindered. Get your means where you can handle it for the benefit of the cause of God. Send your treasures before you into heaven."—5Testimonies, p. 464

"Hear me, O Judah, and ye inhabitants of Jerusalem; Believe in the LORD your God, so shall ye be established; believe his prophets, so shall ye prosper."—II Chronicles 20:20

"I am charged to tell our people, that do not realize, that the devil has device after device, and he carries them out in ways that ***they do not expect****. Satan's agencies will invent ways to make sinners out of saints. I tell you now, that* ***when I am laid to rest, great changes will take place****. I do not know when I shall be taken; and I desire to warn all against the devices of the devil.* ***I want the people to know that I warned them fully before my death."****—Manuscript 1, Feb. 24, 1915*

The Signal to Flee

"Before the destruction of Sodom, God sent a message to Lot, "Escape for thy life; look not behind thee, neither stay thou in all the plain; escape to the mountain, lest thou be consumed." ***The same voice of warning was heard by the disciples of Christ before the destruction of Jerusalem****: 'When ye shall see Jerusalem compassed with armies, then know that the desolation thereof is nigh. Then let them which are in Judea flee to the mountains.' (Luke 21:20, 21) They must not tarry to secure anything from their possessions, but must make the most of the opportunity to escape. There was a coming out, a decided separation from the wicked, an escape for life. So it was in the days of Noah;* ***so with Lot****;* ***so with the disciples prior to the destruction of Jerusalem****; and so it will be in the last days.* ***Again the voice of God is heard in a message of warning****, bidding His people to separate themselves from the prevailing iniquity."—Patriarchs and Prophets, p. 166*

"It is no time now for God's people to be fixing their affections or laying up their treasure in the world. ***The***

time is not far distant**, when, like the early disciples, we shall be forced to seek a refuge in desolate and solitary places.* ***As the siege of Jerusalem by the Roman armies was the signal for flight to the Judean Christians, so the assumption of power on the part of our nation, in the decree enforcing the papal sabbath, will be a warning to us. It will then be time to leave the large cities, preparatory to leaving the smaller ones for retired homes in secluded places among the mountains. *And now, instead of seeking expensive dwellings here, we should be preparing to move to a better country, even a heavenly. Instead of spending our means in self-gratification, we should be studying to economize."—Testimonies, vol.5, pp. 464, 465 (1885). Country Living, p. 32*

The statement above was written in 1885. Three years later, in May 21, 1888, Senator H.W. Blair of New Hampshire, introduced a National Sunday law in Congress known as **Senate Bill 2983**. It coincides with the 1888 Minneapolis Minnesota conference where A.T. Jones and E.J. Waggoner introduced the Righteousness by Faith message. Sister White said, **"Had they accepted the message we would have been in the kingdom two years from that date."**

1888 Message Rejected at Minneapolis, Minnesota

"The conference at Minneapolis was the golden opportunity *for all present to humble the heart before God, and to welcome Jesus as the great instructor: but the stand taken by some at the meeting proved their ruin.* ***They have never seen clearly since, and they never will****; for they persistently cherish the spirit that prevailed there, a wicked criticizing denunciatory spirit....They will be asked in the judgment, 'who required this at your hand, to rise up against the message and the messengers I sent to my people with light, with grace and power? Why have you lifted up your soul against God? Why did you block the way with your perverse spirit? And afterward when the evidence was piled upon evidence,* ***why did you not humble your hearts before God, and repent of your rejection of the message of mercy He has sent you?*** *The Lord has not inspired these* *brethren to resist the truth. He designed that they should be baptized with the Holy Spirit, and be living channels of light to our world, in clear, bright rays."—Paulson Collection, p. 154*

"In 1888 in the General Conference held at Minneapolis, Minnesota, the angel of Rev. 18 came down to his work, and was ridiculed, criticized and rejected. And when the message He brings again swells into a loud cry, it will again be ridiculed, and spoken against and be rejected by the majority."—Taking up a Reproach, by Ellen G. White

"Our first duty, one which we owe to God, to ourselves and to our fellow men, is to obey the laws of God, which include the laws of health."—Testimonies, vol. 3, p. 164

Seventh-day Adventists had long anticipated the passing of a National Sunday law, believing that this is the signal to leave the large cities. Few realized that the sign has already been given! If you wait for the Sunday law to be passed before you start the move for Country Living, you are making a big mistake, and it would be too late. Why? Study prayerfully and seriously the 16 Articles presented by Pope John Paul II on page 69 of this book.

National Sunday Law—Last Act in the Drama

"The substitution of the laws of men for the law of God, the exaltation, by merely human authority, of Sunday in place of the Bible Sabbath, is the ***last act in the drama****. When this substitution becomes universal God will reveal Himself. He will arise in His majesty to shake terribly the earth."—Testimonies, vol. 7, p. 141 [1902]*

"When our nation, in its legislative councils, shall enact laws to bind the consciences of men in regard to their religious privileges, enforcing Sunday observance, and bringing oppressive power to bear against those who keep the seventh-day Sabbath, the law of God will, to all intents and purposes, be made void in our land, ***and national apostasy will be followed by national ruin.****"—7BC 977, (1888), LDE 133*

CHAPTER 5

ANCIENT AND MODERN PARALLELISM

Jesus Wept Over Jerusalem

"What child of Israel could gaze upon the scene without a thrill of joy and admiration? But far other thoughts occupy the mind of Jesus. ***"When He was come near, He beheld the city, and wept over it."*** *[Luke 19:41] Amid the universal rejoicing of the triumphal entry, while palm branches wave, while glad hosannas awake the echoes of the hills, and thousands of voices declare him king, the world's Redeemer is overwhelmed with a sudden and mysterious sorrow. He, the Son of God, the Promised One of Israel, whose power has conquered death, and called its captives from the grave,* ***is in tears,*** *not of ordinary grief, but of intense, irrepressible agony."<4SP 17.2>*

Jesus Wept Over Modern Jerusalem [SDA]

"Christ sorrows and weeps over our churches, over our institutions of learning, that have failed to meet the demand of God. He comes to investigate in Battle Creek, which has been moving in the same track as Jerusalem. The publishing house has been turned into desecrated shrines, into places of unholy merchandise and traffic. It has become a place where injustice and fraud have been carried on, where selfishness, malice, envy, and passion have been borne sway. Yet the men who have led into this working upon wrong principles are seemingly unconscious of their wrong course of action. When warnings and entreaties come to them, they say, doth He not speak in parables? Words of warning and reproof have been treated as idle tales."— Publishing Ministry, p. 167, Letter 31, 1898

"Prophets had wept over the apostasy of Israel. Jeremiah *wished that his eyes were a fountain of tears, that he might "weep day and night for the slain of the daughter of his people." <4SP 20.3>*

The tears that Jesus Christ and His prophets have shed, is a dire warning of a forthcoming doom to modern

Jerusalem [SDA]. When shall His people heed those warnings and entreaties? When shall they learn from the past history of ancient Israel? When shall they recognize that the modern Roman banner has already been planted in modern Jerusalem? When it is too late for them to realize that they have reached the point of no return and there's no other way out but to receive the mark of the beast, in order for them to continue operating their various institutions.

Ellen G. White Wept Over Confiscated Spirit of Prophecy Books

"That night I dreamed that I was in Battle Creek looking out from the side glass at the door and saw a company marching up to the house, two and two. They looked stern and determined. I knew them well and turned to open the parlor door to receive them, but thought I would look again. The scene was changed. ***The company now presented the appearance of a Catholic procession. One bore in his hand a cross, another a reed***. And as

they approached, the one carrying a reed made a circle around the house, saying three times: ***'This house is proscribed. The goods must be confiscated. They have spoken against our holy order.'*** Terror seized me, and I ran through the house, out of the north door, and found myself in the midst of a company, some of whom I knew, but I dared not speak a word to them for fear of being betrayed. I tried to seek a retired spot where I might weep and pray without meeting eager, inquisitive eyes wherever I turned. I repeated frequently: 'If I could only understand this! If they will tell me what I have said or what I have done! ***I wept and prayed much as I saw our goods confiscated.'"***—1T, p. 578

"The very last deception of Satan will be to make none effect the Testimony of the Spirit of God. *'Where there is no vision, the people perish.' Prov. 29:18. Satan will work ingeniously, in different ways and through different agencies, to unsettle the confidence of God's remnant people in the true testimony."—1SM, p. 48*

Modern Israel's Joshua and Caleb

"I saw that ***Jones and Waggoner*** *has their* ***counterpart in Joshua and Caleb.*** *As the children of Israel stoned the spies with literal stones, you have stoned these brethren with stones of sarcasm and ridicule.* ***I saw that you willfully rejected what you know to be truth*** *just because it was too humiliating to your dignity. I saw that some in your tents mimicking and making all manner of fun of these brethren.* ***I also saw that if you had accepted_their message we would have been in the kingdom two years from that***

***date**, but now we have to go back into the wilderness and stay forty years."—Written from Melbourne, Australia, May 9, 1892, by Ellen G. White*

The General Conference in 1888 at Minneapolis, Minnesota was the most important event in the history of Seventh-day Adventist church. Had they accepted the message of Righteousness by Faith preached by A.T. Jones and E.J. Waggoner, and confirmed by Ellen G. White, they would have been in the kingdom two years from that date. It was also in May of that year that Senator H.W. Blair introduced a National Sunday law Bill in the U.S. Congress but was defeated.

*"When do her (Babylon) sin reach unto heaven? [Rev. 18:5] **When the law of God is finally made void by legislation**."—Last Days Event, p.198, Signs of the Times, 6/12/1893*

Babylon had many sins, but there's one particular sin that would trigger the fourth angel of Revelation 18:1-5 to come down and cry out *"Babylon the great is fallen, is fallen.... come out of her my people....for her sins have reached unto heaven and God hath remembered her iniquities."* When the Sabbath of the fourth commandment is substituted by a spurious or false sabbath through a National Sunday law decree, first in America and then universally, then, ***"[It is] time for [thee], LORD, to work:***

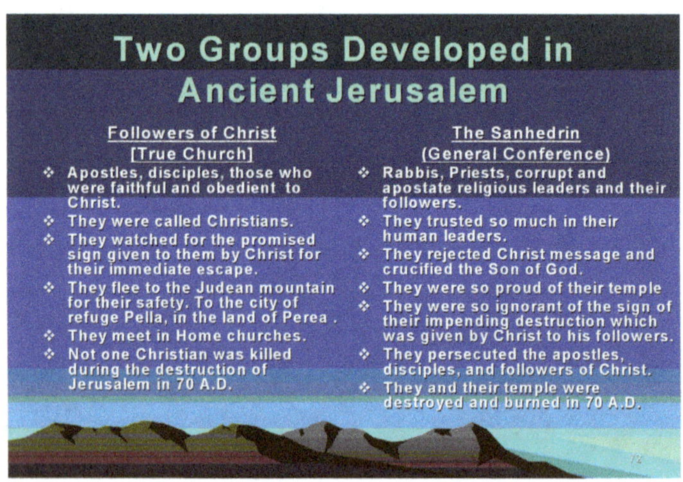

[for] they have made void thy law."—*Psalms 119:126*

"I have been shown that the ***spirit of the world is fast leavening the church. You are following the same path as did ancient Israel.*** *Your neglect to follow light will place you in a more unfavorable position than the Jews upon whom Christ pronounced a woe. (Matt 23) They wish to have Christ as their Saviour, but will not bear the cross and wear His yoke. May the Lord have mercy upon you: for if you go on this way,* ***nothing but evil can be prophesied concerning you.****"—5T, p.75-77*

"Satan is working that the ***history of the Jewish nation may be repeated*** *in the experience of those who believe* ***present truth."***—*2 Selected Messages, p. 111*

"Satan is continually seeking to overcome the people of God by breaking down the barriers which separate them from the world. ***Ancient Israel*** *was enticed into sin when they ventured into forbidden association with the heathen. In a similar manner are* ***modern Israel*** *led astray. "The god of this world hath blinded the minds of them which believe not, lest the light of the glorious gospel of Christ, who is the image of God, should shine unto them." 2 Corinthians 4:4* ***All who are not decided followers of Christ are servants of Satan."***—*Great Controversy, p. 509*

A Lesson for Modern Israel

"Please read the third chapter [of Jeremiah]. ***This chapter is a lesson for modern Israel.*** *Let all who claim to be children of God understand that He will not serve with their sins any more than He would with the sins of* ***ancient Israel****. God hates hereditary and cultivated tendencies to wrong."—(Letter 34, 1899) {4BC 1154.9}*

"I was pointed back to ancient Israel. ***But two of the adults*** *of the vast army that left Egypt* ***entered the land of Canaan.*** *Their dead bodies were strewn in the wilderness because of their transgressions.* ***Modern Israel is in greater danger of forgetting God and being led into idolatry than were His ancient people****. Many idols are worshiped, even by professed Sabbath-keepers. God especially charged His ancient people to guard against idolatry, for if they should be led away from serving the living God, His curse would*

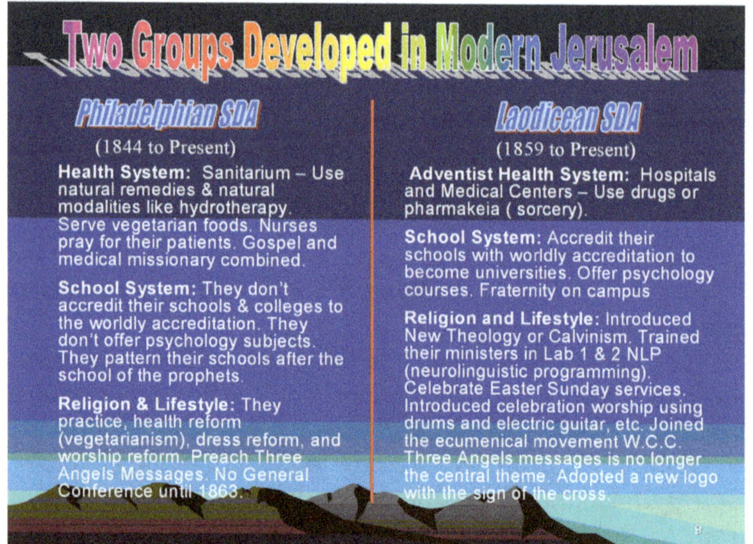

rest upon them, while if they would love Him with all their heart, with all their soul, and with all their might, He would abundantly bless them in basket and in store, and would remove sickness from the midst of them."—1 Testimonies, p. 609

"The people are encouraged to center in Battle Creek, and they pay their tithe and give their influence to the building up of ***a modern Jerusalem that is not after God's order****. In this work other places are cut off from facilities which they should have. Enlarge ye, spread, yes; but not in one place. Go out and establish centers of influence in places where nothing, or next to nothing, has been done. Break up your consolidated mass; diffuse the saving beams of light, and shed light into the darkened corners of the earth." —Testimonies to Ministers, pp. 254, 255 (1895) Country Living, p. 24*

CHAPTER 6

MODERN JERUSALEM NOT BABYLON

"Mark the whole tenor of this chapter, and learn the lesson it conveys to **modern Israel [SDA].** *These things are written for our ensamples upon whom the ends of the world are come. We see the unbelief, and the stout resistance of some who have had great light, and although evidence has been piled upon evidence, they have kept themselves in stubborn resistance. The Lord has sent messages of warning and entreaty, messages of reproof and rebuke, and they have not been in vain. But we have never had a message that the Lord would disorganize the church.* ***We have never had the prophecy concerning Babylon applied to the Seventh-day Adventist Church,*** *or been informed that the "loud cry" consisted in calling God's people to come out of her; for* ***this is not God's plan concerning [Modern] Israel****....Now can we expect that a message would be true that would designate as Babylon the people for whom God has done so much? Hell would triumph should such a message be received, and the world would be strengthened in iniquity." —Review and Herald, vol. 3, p. 86, October 03, 1893 [Emphasis supplied] 2 Selected Messages, p. 68*

"Those who have published the "Loud Cry" tract have not consulted me upon the subject. They have quoted largely from my writings and put their own construction upon them. They claim to have a special message from God to pronounce the Seventh-day Adventist Church Babylon, proclaim her fall, and call the people of God to come out of her, ***and try to make the testimonies substantiate their theory.*** *These publications are misleading minds, and increasing the prejudice already existing, and tend to make it more difficult to get access to them to present the message God has given in warnings to the world of altogether a different character from the ideas presented in these pamphlets." —1 Manuscript Release, p. 348*

"For years I have borne my testimony to the effect that when any one arises claiming to have great light, and

yet advocating the tearing down of that which the Lord through His human agents has been building up, they are greatly deceived, and are not working along the lines where Christ is working. ***Those who assert that the Seventh-day Adventist churches constitute Babylon, or any part of Babylon, might better stay at home.*** *" —Review and Herald, Aug. 22, 1893*

"When men arise, claiming to have a message from God, but instead of warring against principalities and powers, and the rulers of darkness of this world, they form a hallow square, and turn the weapons of warfare against church militant, be afraid of them. ***They do not bear the divine credentials.*** *God has not given them any such burden of labor.* ***They would tear down that which God would restore by the Laodicean message."*** *—Testimonies to Ministers, p. 22*

Some brethren from the home church, and splintered groups would call the Seventh-day Adventist church Babylon. They should examine the above statements with humbleness of heart and mind and the rest of the quotations that attest to the fact that the Seventh-day Adventist church is not Babylon per se, but rather modern Israel or modern Jerusalem. It's true that the SDA church has been in the Laodicean condition since 1859 as recorded in Notebook Leaflets, page 99. ***"The Church is in the <u>Laodicean state</u>. The presence of God is not in her midst."***

The message that will restore the Laodicean SDA to God's favor is the Laodicean Message.

"God is leading out a people. He has a chosen people, a church on the earth, whom He has made the depositaries of His law. He has committed to them sacred trust and eternal truth to be given to the world. He would reprove and correct them. ***The message to the Laodiceans is applicable to Seventh-day Adventists who have had great light and have not walked in the light****. It is those who have made great profession, but have not kept in step with their Leader, that will be spewed out of His mouth unless they repent.* ***The message to pronounce the Seventh-Day Adventist Church Babylon, and call the people of God out of her,***

does not come from any heavenly messenger, or any human agent inspired by the Spirit of God*. The True Witness says, "I counsel thee to buy of me gold tried in the fire, that thou mayest be rich; and white raiment, that thou mayest be clothed, and that the shame of thy nakedness do not appear; and anoint thine eyes with eyesalve, that thou mayest see. As many as I love, I rebuke and chasten: be zealous therefore, and repent. Behold, I stand at the door, and knock; if any man hear my voice, and open the door, I will come in to him, and will sup with him, and he with me. To him that overcometh will I grant to sit with me in my throne, even as I also overcame, and am set down with my Father in his throne" (Rev. 3:18-21)" —2SM, p. 67*

"Beware of those who arise with great burden to denounce the church. The chosen ones who are standing and breasting the storm of opposition from the world, and are uplifting the downtrodden commandments of God to exalt them as holy and honorable, are indeed the light of the world. How dare mortal man pass his judgment upon them and call the church harlot, Babylon, a den of thieves, a cage of every unclean and hateful bird, the habitation of devils, making the nations drunk with the wine of her fornication, confederating with the kings and great men of the earth, waxing rich through the abundance of her delicacies, and proclaiming that her sins have reached unto heaven and God hath remembered her iniquities? ***Is this the message we are to bear to Seventh-day Adventist? I tell you, no! God has given no man such message****. Let these men humble their hearts before God, and in true contrition repent that they have even for a time stood by the side of the accuser of the brethren who accused them before God day and night..." —This Day with God, p. 172*

"Dear Brother M: *Your letter addressed to me was received at the beginning of the Sabbath.... I should advise you to attend the school, and not to leave this country until you become thoroughly settled in your mind as to what is truth. I sincerely hope that you will attend this term of school and learn all you can in regard to this message of truth that is to go to the world." —2 Selected Messages, p. 63.1*

"The Lord has not given you a message to call the Seventh-day Adventists Babylon, and to call the people of God to come out of her. *All the reasons you may present cannot have weight with me on this subject, because the Lord has given me decided light that is opposed to such a message." —2 Selected Messages, p. 63.2*

"I do not doubt your sincerity or honesty. I have written long letters at different times to those who were accusing the church of Seventh-day Adventists of being Babylon, that they were not handling the truth. You think individuals have prejudiced my mind. If I am in this state, I am not fitted to be entrusted with the work of God. But this matter has been brought before my mind in other cases where individuals have claimed to have messages for the Seventh-day Adventist Church, of a similar character, and the word has been given me, **"Believe them not." "I have not sent them, and yet they ran."** *—2 Selected Messages, p. 63*

"Napier, New Zealand, March 23, 1893. **"Dear Brother S.:** *"I address to you a few lines. I am not in harmony with the position that you have taken, for I have been shown by the Lord that just such positions will be taken by those who are in error. Paul has given us warning to this effect: 'Now the Spirit speaketh expressly, that in the latter times some shall depart from the faith, giving heed to seducing spirits, and doctrines of devils." —Testimonies to Ministers, p. 58*

"My brother, I learn that you are taking the position that the Seventh-day Adventist Church is Babylon, and that all that would be saved must come out of her. You are not the only man the devil has deceived in this matter. For the last forty years, one man after another has arisen, claiming that the Lord has sent him with the same message; but let me tell you, as I have told them, that this message you are proclaiming is one of the satanic delusions designed to create confusion among the churches." —Testimonies to Ministers, p. 58

"My brother, you are certainly off the track. The second angel's message was to go to Babylon [the churches] proclaiming her downfall, and calling the people to come out of her. This same message is to be proclaimed the second time.... ***"My brother, if you are teaching that the Seventh-***

day Adventist Church is Babylon, you are wrong, God has not given you any such message to bear*. Satan will use every mind to which he can attain access, inspiring men to originate false theories or go off on some wrong tangent, that he may create a false excitement, and thus divert souls from the true issue for this time. I presume that some may be deceived by your message, because they are full of curiosity and desire for some new thing." —Testimonies to Ministers, p. 59*

How Does the Church Convert Into Babylon?

"It is our individual duty to walk humbly with God. We are not to seek any strange, new message. We are not to think that the chosen ones of God who are trying to walk in the light, compose Babylon. The fallen denominational churches are Babylon. Babylon has been fostering poisonous doctrines, the wine of error. ***This wine of error is made up of false doctrines****, such as (1)* ***the natural immortality of the soul****, (2)* ***the eternal torment of the wicked****, (3)* ***the denial of the pre-existence of Christ prior to His birth in Bethlehem****, and (4)* ***advocating and exalting the first day of the week above God's holy, sanctified day****. These and kindred errors are presented to the world by the various churches. . . ."— Evangelism ,p.365, Review and Herald, Sept. 12, 1893*

The Seventh-day Adventist Reform Movement has a teaching that the Seventh-day Adventist Church is Babylon. It is unfair to stereo-type those Seventh-day Adventists who are trying their best to practice health reform, Sabbath reform, dress reform and worship reform, and be called "**reform**" and be classified with the SDARM, and hate them because they call the SDA church Babylon. It is sad to note that when the real message of revival and reformation is presented, they are as close as a clam and prejudiced by their preconceived ideas.

It cannot be denied that there are more than a dozen groups who have separated from the mainline Seventh-day Adventist church. We have the Branch Davidians, Shepherd's Rod, Elijah Movement, SDA Wilderness, Creation 7th-day Adventist, Seventh-day Sabbath Church, Historic SDA, Seventh-Day Adventist Reform Movement,

Seventh-day Adventist Reform Church, Bible Sabbath Fellowship of SDA, to name a few. These are professing Seventh-day Adventists, keeping the Sabbath, but just like the mainline Adventist, they are not following the exact blueprint given by God to modern Jerusalem/Israel. *"Let church members bear in mind that the fact that their names are registered on the church books will not save them." —9 Testimonies, p. 47-48.*

Most of them call the mainline SDA church Babylon, but if ask the question "what are you now?" they would say Seventh-day Adventist. Therefore, you are also Babylon? Then, they would deny it.

The Name that God has Given Us

"We are Seventh-day Adventists. Are we ashamed of our name? We answer, No, no! *We are not.* ***It is the name the Lord has given us.*** *It points out the truth that is to be the test of the churches. That this may be, we must look ever to Jesus.*

"The name Seventh-day Adventist carries the true features of our faith in front, and will convict the inquiring mind. Like an arrow from the Lord's quiver, it will wound the transgressors of God's law, and will lead to repentance toward God and faith in our Lord Jesus Christ." —Faith I Live By, p. 304

The name Baptist, Methodist, Pentecostal, Jehovah's Witness, Mormon, etc, are names given by men, not by God.

Standing Rebuke to Protestant World

"The name Seventh-day Adventist is a standing rebuke to the Protestant world. Here is the line of distinction between the worshipers of God and those who worship the beast and receive his mark." —1 Testimonies, p. 223

Will Make the Name Less Prominent

Time will come when the name Seventh-day Adventist will be made less prominent. When we first moved to San Diego, California in 1996, we attended the SDA church in La Mesa. The name was, "La Mesa Seventh-day Adventist Church." At present, it was changed to **"La**

Mesa Adventist Community Church." I am not predicting but based on the quotation below, more and more SDA church will remove the name "Seventh-day" and just use Adventist. Any body who believes in the second coming of Jesus is considered "Adventist" but not necessarily a Sabbath-keeper.

*"Men will employ every means to make less prominent the difference between Seventh-day Adventists and observers of the first day of the week. A company was presented before me under the name of Seventh-day Adventists, who were advising that the banner, or sign, which makes us a distinct people should **not** be held out so strikingly; for they claimed that this was not the best policy in order to secure success to our institutions. But this is not a time to haul down our colors, to be ashamed of our faith. This distinctive banner, described in the words, "Here is the patience of the saints: here are they that keep the commandments of God, and the faith of Jesus," is to be borne through the world to the close of probation." —6 Testimonies, p. 144*

Spiritual Quality, Not Quantity

*"If you **lower the standard in order to secure popularity and an increase of numbers**, and then make this increase a cause of rejoicing, you show great blindness. If numbers were evidence of success, Satan might claim the pre-eminence, for in this world his followers are largely in the majority. It is the degree of moral power pervading the college that is a test of its prosperity. It is the virtue, intelligence, and piety of the people composing our churches, not their numbers that should be a source of joy and thankfulness." —5 Testimonies, p. 31-32*

"As our numbers are increasing, broader plans must be laid to meet the increasing demands of the times; but we see no special increase of fervent piety, of Christian simplicity, and earnest devotion. The church seems content to take only the first steps in conversion. They are more ready for active labor than for humble devotion, more ready to engage in outward religious service than in the inner work of the heart. Meditation and prayer are neglected for bustle and show. Religion must begin with

emptying and purifying the heart, and must be nurtured by daily prayer.

"The steady progress of our work, and our increased facilities, are filling the hearts and minds of many of our people with satisfaction and pride, which we fear will take the place of the love of God in the soul. Busy activity in the mechanical part of even the work of God may so occupy the mind that prayer shall be neglected, and self-importance and self-sufficiency, so ready to urge their way, shall take the place of true goodness, meekness, and lowliness of heart. The zealous cry may be heard: "The temple of the Lord, The temple of the Lord, are these." "Come with me, and see my zeal for the Lord." But where are the burden bearers?" —4 Testimonies, p. 535

CHAPTER 7

PHILADELPHIAN SDA VS. LAODICEAN SDA

"Now was seen the application of those words of Christ in the Revelation, addressed to the church at this very time: "These things saith He that is holy, He that is true, He that hath the key of David, He that openeth, and no man shutteth; and shutteth, and no man openeth; I know thy works: behold, ***I have set before thee an open door, and no man can shut it."*** *—Great Controversy, p. 430*

The church addressed to here is the Philadelphian church (Rev. 3:7-13) in 1844. But instead of walking the straight and narrow path, in 1859, they turned away (shoot off) from the original blue print given by God to the Seventh-day Adventist church, and became Laodicean SDA, as illustrated in the diagram. They didn't follow the Lamb in the most holy.

"They now saw that they were correct in believing that the end of the 2300 days in 1844 marked an important crisis. But while it was true that that door of hope and mercy by which men had for eighteen hundred years found access to God, was closed, another door was opened, and forgiveness of sins was offered to men through the intercession of Christ

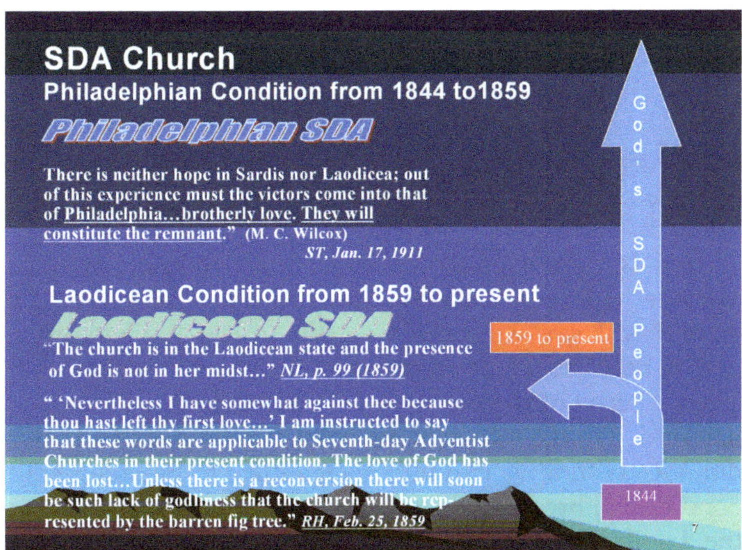

in the most holy. One part of His ministration had closed, only to give place to another. There was still an "open door" to the heavenly sanctuary, where Christ was ministering in the sinner's behalf." —Great Controversy, p. 429.

Those who came out from the various denominations in 1844 as a result of William Miller's preaching were about 50,000. Shortly after the great disappointment, majority returned to the churches they came from and only 50 remained which composed the early SDA pioneers. Among them were, Ellen G. White, James White, Hiram Edson, Joseph Bates, Frederick Wheeler, Charles Fitch, and Rachel Oakes, a Seventh-day Baptist who introduced the group into Sabbath keeping. The church that the early pioneers started in 1844 was in the Philadelphian condition as recorded in Revelation 3:7-8. In 1859 the messenger of God declared *that* ***"The church is in the Laodicean state and the presence of God is not in her midst."*** *—Notebook Leaflets, p. 99*

That's why Jesus Christ said ***"'nevertheless I have somewhat against thee because thou hast left thy first love...'*** *I am instructed to say that these words are applicable to Seventh day Adventist Churches in their present [Laodicean] condition. The love of God has been lost...Unless there is a reconversion there will soon be such lack of godliness that the church will be represented by the barren fig tree." —Review and Herald, Feb. 25, 1859*

They have left the Philadelphian condition of brotherly love. They have put Jesus outside the church. *"Behold, I stand at the door, and knock: if any man hear my voice, and open the door, I will come in to him, and will sup with him, and he with me." —Rev. 3:20*

God is calling us to return to the condition or state of Philadelphia—brotherly love, the sixth church. Some people will say we cannot return to the Philadelphian period because we are already in the seventh—Laodicea. **The real crux of the matter is in understanding what God has said.** He did not say period but condition or state. He did not say that we can no longer return to Philadelphian condition of brotherly love. Maybe somebody has said that the Laodicean SDA is the remnant church and will go through the sea of glass, God never said that. As a matter of fact, Jesus is knocking day and night at the door of our individual hearts, pleading and wanting to come in and sup with us. Here is God's simple solution to the Laodicean SDA problem. Escape from the Laodicean SDA condition and return to the Philadelphian SDA condition.

"There is neither hope in Sardis nor Laodicea; out of this experience must the victors come into that of Philadelphia... brotherly love. He has no promise for Laodicea as a whole (corporately)... ***but the individual who opens the heart's door and lets Christ in, who comes into that wonderful communion with the divine Lord, will by that very process come into the condition of brotherly love (Philadelphia). They will constitute the remnant."*** *—(M.C. Wilcox) Signs of the Times, Jan. 17, 1911*

We have to return to the original blueprint that God has given to His last day church. We need revival and reformation among the SDA churches.

"And if ***ye will not be reformed by me*** *by these things, but will walk contrary unto me; Then will I also walk contrary unto you,* ***and will punish you yet seven times for your sins****. And I will bring a sword upon you, that shall avenge the quarrel of [my] covenant: and when ye are gathered together within your cities, I will send the pestilence among you; and ye shall be delivered into the hand of the enemy." —Leviticus 26:23-25*

Laodicean Condition-Sick and Dying

"The church, in its present condition is declared to be in the ***Laodicean state*** *and like a vast hospital with the sick and dying...which material prosperity has attended our work, we have as a people, been retreating toward the world spiritually. Spiritual progress is the only kind that God recognizes. If numbers were evidence of success, Satan might claim the preeminence...it is virtue, intelligence and piety of the people composing our churches, not their numbers that should be a source of joy and thankfulness." —Review and Herald, Feb 25, 1902*

"The state of the church represented by the foolish virgins is also spoken of as the Laodicean state. *The True Witness* *declares, "I know thy works, that thou art neither cold nor hot: I would that thou wert cold or hot. So then because thou art lukewarm, and neither cold nor hot,* ***I will spew thee out of my mouth."*** *—Review & Herald, Volume 2, August 19, 1890*

"The message to the Laodiceans is applicable to Seventh-day Adventists who have had great light and have not walked in the light*. It is those who have made great profession, but have not kept in step with their Leader, that will be spewed out of His mouth unless they repent." —2 Selected Messages, p. 67*

Figure of Spewing Out

"To those who are indifferent at this time Christ's warning is: "Because thou art lukewarm, and neither cold nor hot, I will spew thee out of My mouth." —Revelation 3:16 The figure of spewing out of His mouth means that (1) ***He cannot offer up your prayers or your expressions of love to God.*** *(2)****He cannot endorse your teaching of His word or your spiritual work in anywise.*** *(3)* ***He cannot present your religious exercises with the request that grace be given you."*** *—6 Testimonies, p. 408.*

Philadelphian SDA-True Church of the Last Days

"Now just as sure as the ***Philadelphian church is the true church of the last days****, just as sure the 144,000 are sealed, just before the coming of the Lord." —Review and Herald, May 9, 1854*

"The 144,000 were all sealed and perfectly united. On their foreheads was written God, New Jerusalem, and a glorious star containing Jesus' new name." —Early Writings, p. 15

"And I looked, and, lo, a lamb stood on the mount Sion, and with Him an hundred and forty four thousand, having His Father's name written in their foreheads." —Revelation 14:1

Shaking Among the SDA Churches

"I asked the meaning of the shaking I had seen and was shown that it would be caused by the ***straight testimony*** *called forth by the counsel of the True Witness to the Laodiceans. This will have its effect upon the heart of the receiver, and will lead him to exalt the standard and pour forth the straight*

truth. ***Some will not bear this straight testimony. They will rise up against it*** *and this is what will cause a shaking among God's people." —Early Writings, 270*

Rejection of Testimonies Leads to Open Rebellion

"It is Satan's plan to weaken the faith of God's people in the Testimonies. Next follows skepticism in regard to the vital points of our faith, the pillars of our position, then doubt as to the Holy Scriptures, and then the downward march to perdition. When the Testimonies, which were once believed, are doubted and given up, Satan knows the deceived ones will not stop at this; and he redoubles his efforts till he launches them into open rebellion, which becomes incurable and ends in destruction." —4 Testimonies, p. 211

Professed Adventist Will Bow at Saints Feet

"You think, that those who worship before the saint's feet, (Philadelphian SDA-Rev3:9), will at last be saved. Here I must differ with you; for God showed me that these classes were ***professed Adventist (Laodicean),*** *who had fallen away, and "crucified to themselves the Son of God afresh, and put Him to an open shame." And in the "hour of temptation." which is yet to come, to show out every one's true character,* ***they will know that they are forever lost;*** *and overwhelmed with anguish of spirit, they will bow at the saint's feet." —Words to the Little Flock, p.12*

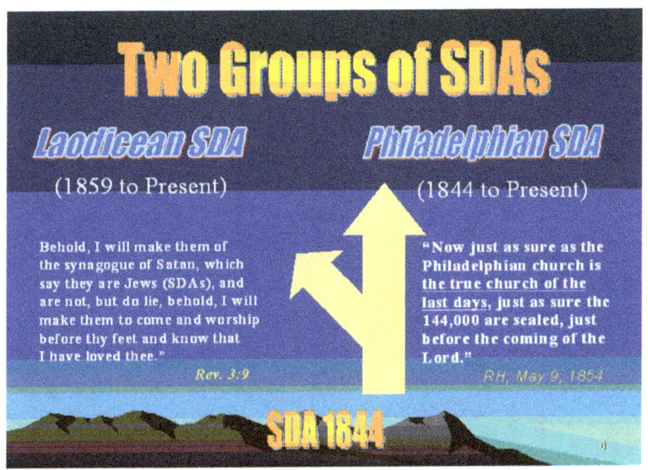

False Reformation in Modern Jerusalem-SDA

"The enemy of souls has sought to bring in the supposition that a great reformation was to take place among Seventh-day Adventists, and that this reformation would consist in [A] giving up the doctrines which stand as the pillars of our faith, and [B] engaging in a process of reorganization. Were these reformations to take place, what would result? [1] The principles of truth that God in His wisdom has given to the remnant church, would be discarded. [2] Our religion would be changed. [3] The fundamental principles that have sustained the work for the last fifty years would be accounted as error. [4] A new organization would be established. [5] Books of a new order would be written. [6] A system of intellectual philosophy would be introduced. [7] The founders of this system would go into the cities, and do a wonderful work. [8] The Sabbath of course, would be lightly regarded, as [9] also the God who created it. [10] Nothing would be allowed to stand in the way of the new movement. [11] The leaders would teach that virtue is better than vice, but God being removed, [12] they would place their dependence on human power, which, without God, is worthless. [13] Their foundation would be built on the sand, and storm and tempest would sweep away the structure." —1 Selected Messages, p. 204.2 (1904) This is a fulfilled prophecy by EGW.

"Let none seek to tear away the foundations of our faith—the foundations that were laid at the beginning of our work [1844], by prayerful study of the Word and by revelation. ***Upon these foundations we have been building for more than fifty years.*** *Men may suppose that they have found a new way, that they can lay a stronger foundation than that which has been laid; but this is a great deception. "Other foundation can no man lay than that is laid." [1 COR. 3:11] In the past, many have undertaken to build a new faith, to establish new principles; but how long did their building stand? It soon fell; for it was not founded upon the Rock." —Gospel Workers, p. 307*

"In a representation which passed before me, I saw a certain work being done by medical missionary workers. Our ministering brethren were looking on, watching what

*was being done, but they did not seem to understand. The foundation of our faith, which was established by so much prayer, such earnest searching of the Scriptures, was being taken down, pillar by pillar. Our faith was to have nothing to rest upon—**the sanctuary was gone, the atonement was gone....**"—The Upward Look, p.152*

If you compare old Adventism with the present, it's far different. But the true remnant—Philadelphian SDA, will stick to God's original blue print, the doctrines that are contained in the Bible and Spirit of Prophecy. In the SDA 27 Fundamental Beliefs, now 28, it states that the **atonement was finished on the cross.** On the contrary, the **atonement begun on the cross** and will be completed in the Heavenly Sanctuary above. Christ was the final sacrifice, the Lamb of God which taketh away the sins of the world. Final atonement could only be done by our High Priest in the Most Holy place in the Sanctuary above.

"The intercession of Christ in man's behalf in the Sanctuary above is as essential to the plan of salvation as was His death upon the cross. **By His death He began that work which after His resurrection He ascended to complete in heaven."** —Great Controversy, p. 489

Following Jesus Christ in the Most Holy Place

"Those who rose up with Jesus would send up their faith to Him in the holiest, and pray, "My Father, give us Thy Spirit." Then Jesus would breathe upon them the Holy Ghost. In that breath was light, power, and much love, joy, and peace.

*"I turned to look at the company who were still bowed before the throne; **they did not know that Jesus had left it.***

Satan appeared to be on the throne, would then breathe upon them unholy influence, in it there was light and much power, but no sweet love, joy, and peace	Jesus Christ our High Priest would breathe upon them the Holy Ghost, with light, power, and much love, joy, and peace.
Holy Place	**Most Holy Place**

Satan appeared to be by the throne, trying to carry on the work of God. I saw them look up to the throne, and pray, "Father, give us Thy Spirit." Satan would then breathe upon them an unholy influence; in it there was light and much power, but no sweet love, joy, and peace. Satan's object was to keep them deceived and to draw back and deceive God's children." —Early Writings, p. 55

CHAPTER 8

THE NEW WORLD ORDER [EXCERPTS FROM BOB TREFZ "FREEDOM'S RING" VOLUME 1, NO. 1 & 2]

"Willing or not, ready or not, we are all involved in an all-out, no-holds-barred, three-way global competition. Most of us are not competitors, however. We are the stakes. For the competition is about who will establish **the first one world system of the government** that has ever existed in the society of nations....The competition is all-out because, now that it has started, there is no way it can be reversed or called off." —Malachi Martin, a Jesuit and Vatican insider, Keys of This Blood, p. 15

The world and all that's in it—our way of life as individuals and as citizens of the nation; our families and jobs; our trade, commerce, and money; our educational systems, our religions and cultures; even the badges of our national identity, which most of us have always taken for granted—**all will have been powerfully and radically altered forever.** No one can be exempted from its effects. No sector of our lives will remain untouched.

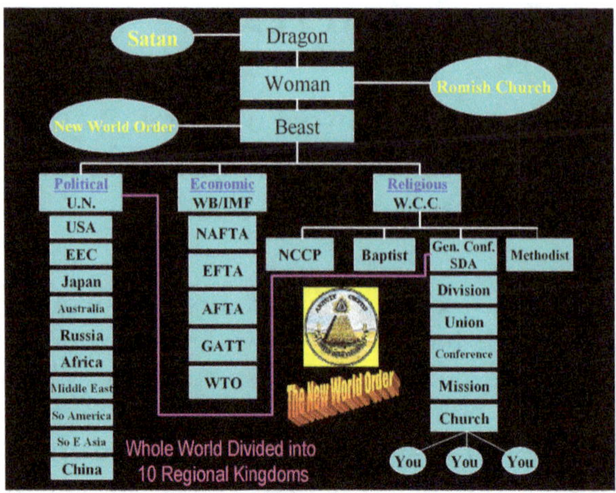

"The scriptures teaches that popery is to regain its lost supremacy, and that the fires of persecution will be rekindled through the time-serving concessions of the so-called Protestant world." —2 Selected Messages, pp. 367-368

"In the seventeenth of Revelation is foretold the destruction of all churches who corrupt themselves by idolatrous devotion to the service of the papacy, those who have drunk of the wine of the wrath of her fornication. [Rev. 17:1-4 quoted]. Thus is represented the papal power, which with all deceivableness of unrighteousness, by outside attraction and gorgeous display, <u>deceives all nations</u>: promising them, as did Satan our first parents, all good to those who receive its mark, and all harm to those who oppose its fallacies." — (Letter 232, 1899) Vol. 7A SDA Bible Commentary.

"And the dragon gave him his power, and his seat, and great authority." —Rev. 13:2

***"And shall give their power and strength unto the beast."** —Rev. 17:13 Comment the Spirit of Prophecy, "These have one mind." There will be a universal bond of union, one great harmony, a confederacy of Satan's force." —MS 24, 1891 (SDABC, vol. 7a, p.98.3)*

The perspective of John Paul II, according to Malachi Martin, with respect to groups such as Seventh-day Adventists is as follows: **Adventist was formed, according to him, in a context of rebellion against the authority and privileged teaching power of the Roman Church**. Having clambered off the triumphal "advancing geo-religious caravan" of the papal church, Adventism has remained its deep objections to the authority and person of John Paul.

United Nations–The Political Arm of the New World Order

The United Nations, which is the political arm of the Papal New World Order, has its office inside the General Conference of Seventh-day Adventist in Silver Spring, Maryland. Evidently, it shows that the SDA church is directly and actively involved with the various functions of the U.N., a Church and State consortium. This is not only being an observer, but becoming a part of it. The U.N. will unite the whole world politically under the pretext of achieving peace and harmony. On the contrary, this is the very agency that Satan will use to force God's people to obey its oppressive edicts under the pain of death. *"And it was given unto him to make war with the saints, and to overcome them: and power was given him over all kindred, and tongues, and nations." —Rev. 13:7 "And cause that as many as would not worship the image of the beast should be killed." —Rev. 13:15*

U.N. Office inside the General Conference of SDA

"Ye adulterers and adulteresses, know ye not that ***the friendship of the world is enmity with God?*** *whosoever therefore will be* ***a friend of the world is the enemy of God."*** *—James 4:4*

John Paul Predicts Roman Catholic Absorption of Adventism

As John Paul casts his eye upon this rebelliousness, he takes the position that Adventism does "contain some parts of the full revelation made by God to His Church, which he placed under Peter's care. On the Day of Reward and Retribution for which each of this groups (including Adventism) waits, whatever elements of true religion each maintains will surely be integrated into a profession of the full faith of Christ." —Keys of This Blood, p. 287

Looking carefully at those statements from the perspective of Roman Catholic theology (which definitely has no scenario of end time events like ours) and the way in which Malachi Martin defines his terms internally and contextually, John Paul believes that Roman Catholicism will absorb Seventh-day Adventism.

Exhibit #3 - Brochure published by the GC sponsored "La Voz De La Esperanza"

En El "Vaticano" Adventista?

Neal C. Wilson, former president of the General Conference of Seventh-day Adventists was quoted saying, "there is another universal and truly catholic organization, the Seventh-day Adventist Church." —Adventist Review, March 5, 1981, p. 3

Eliminating Resistance to Rome's Teaching Authority

Ecumenism and Celebration are Vatican's answers to eliminate that rebellion against her privileged teaching authority. Ecumenism eliminates resistance to Rome. Celebration integrates liturgically the thinking and practice of the churches with Rome.

Weapon of Destruction

The use of the Celebration movement in the local church as a political force to unite the worldly element in squeezing out the faithful historic Adventists. The training of leadership in mind control hypnosis using Neuro-Linguistic Programming to control congregations and individuals. The well coordinated promotion of the celebration movement. The timing of the trade marking of the denominational name and the initiation of the trademark lawsuits. The education of our ministry in celebration. Our membership in national branches of the Jesuit theologically-fashioned World Council of Churches. The cozying up to Rome. Taken together, all point to something more than a haphazard worldliness that has come in. **We are facing a well-organized, systematic attempt to erase what still remains of Historic Adventism.**

From Rome: Conform or Become Extinct

Indeed, John Paul holds that such groups as **Adventism "are destined to undergo a series of severe shocks and mutations** as, willy-nilly, they adapt themselves to the new globalism emanating from more powerful groups. There is no way that any one of them [groups differing with Rome] will be able to maintain itself in any vibrancy and progressive strength unless it allows – or suffers – its provincialism to be enlarged beyond the confines it traditionally observed. Individuals among them may for a while maintain themselves within those confines. But inevitably, as groups they will have to face dire alternatives. Either they will become thoroughly and realistically globalize, and therefore capable of collaborating in the building of a geopolitical structure. Or, as groups, they will remain in place, diminish in numbers and influence,

and finally lose their identity as operatives in a new world order." —Keys of This Blood, pp. 291- 292

What is John Paul II Saying? Adventism must conform to his papal new world order or become extinct. True Biblical Adventism will neither conform nor become extinct. *It will, amidst the fiercest persecution ever waged, receive the power of the latter rain, give the loud cry, and walk in the glory that shines from the throne of God.*

Anti-Popery Stanch Consigned to Historical Trash Heap

"Let no man deceive you by any means: *for [that day shall not come], except there come a falling away first,* ***and that***

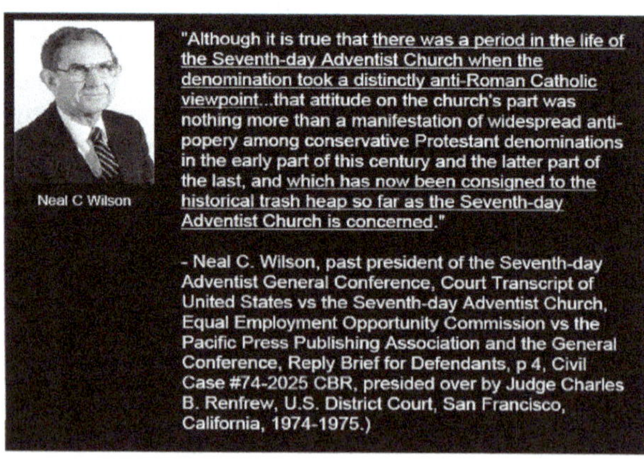

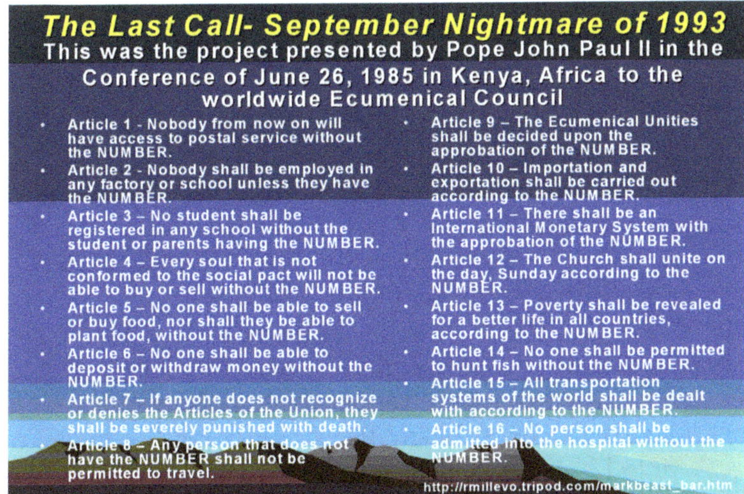

man of sin be revealed, *the son of perdition; Who opposeth and exalteth himself above all that is called God, or that is worshipped; so that he as God sitteth in the temple of God, showing himself that he is God." —2 Thessalonians, 2:3-4*

Political, Economic and Religious Boycott

Here are the Sixteen Articles presented by Pope John Paul II in Kenya, Africa that could affect you and your loved ones lives spiritually and physically. Study it prayerfully and carefully so that you will be able to prepare for what is to come as an overwhelming surprise to the whole wide world.

Article 1 - Nobody from now on will have access to postal service without the NUMBER.

Article 2 - Nobody shall be employed in any factory or school unless they have the NUMBER.

Article 3 – No student shall be registered in any school without the student or parents having the NUMBER.

Article 4 – Every soul that is not conformed to the social pact will not be able to buy or sell without the NUMBER.

Article 5 – No one shall be able to sell or buy food, nor shall they be able to plant food, without the NUMBER.

Article 6 – No one shall be able to deposit or withdraw money without the NUMBER.

Article 7 – If anyone does not recognize or denies the Articles of the Union, they shall be severely punished with death.

Article 8 – Any person that does not have the NUMBER shall not be permitted to travel.

Article 9 – The Ecumenical Unities shall be decided upon the approbation of the NUMBER.

Article 10 – Importation and exportation shall be carried out according to the NUMBER.

Article 11 – There shall be an International Monetary System with the approbation of the NUMBER.

Article 12 – The Church shall unite on the day, Sunday according to the NUMBER.

Article 13 – Poverty shall be revealed for a better life in all countries, according to the NUMBER.

Article 14 – No one shall be permitted to hunt fish without the NUMBER.

Article 15 – All transportation systems of the world shall be dealt with according to the NUMBER.

Article 16 – No person shall be admitted into the hospital without the NUMBER.

Executive Orders Signed Into Law

Below are a series of Executive Orders signed into law by President William J. Clinton on July 16, 1996. The Executive Order # 13010 (Critical Infrastructure Protection) I believe is the pinnacle of the following E.O. #s which states that in the event of a National Emergency *"The Department of Defense shall perform the functions of the President"* You ask, "Why should this bother me? I'm just your average American citizen." According to U.S. Representative Henry Gonzales [Texas], *"All the laws are already on the books to legally make the U.S.A. a dictatorship."* That's right people, all that's needed for the prophecy of enforcing the mark of the beast to be fulfilled is a *"National Emergency."*

When this National Emergency becomes a reality, you will find the following *"Executive Orders"* to be enacted on every man, woman and child in this great land of ours.

E. O. #10995--Seizure of all communications media in the U.S. by the Federal Government.
E. O. #10997--Seizure of all electric power, fuels, and minerals, both public and private by the Federal Government.
E. O. #1098--Seizure of all food supplies and resources, public and private, all farms and farm equipment by the Federal Government.
E. O. #10999--Seizure of all means of transportation, including personal cars, trucks, or vehicles of any kind and total control over all highways, seaports and waterways by the Federal Government.
E. O. #11000--Seizure of all American people for work forces under federal supervision, including the splitting up of families if the government has to.
E. O. #11001--Seizure of all health, education and welfare, facilities both public and private by the Federal Government.
E.O. #11002--Empowers the Postmaster General to register all men, women, and children in the Federal Government.
E.O. #11003--Seizure of all airports and aircraft by the Federal Government
E. O. #11004--Seizure of all housing and finance authorities, to establish forced relocation. Designates areas be abandoned *"unsafe,"* establishes new locations for populations, relocates communities, build new housing with public funds.
E. O. #11005--Seizure of all railroads, inland waterways and storage facilities, both private and public by Federal Government.
E. O. #11051--Provides the Office of Emergency Planning (F.E.M.A.), complete authorization to put the orders into effect in times of increased tension or economic or financial crisis.
E. O. #13010--Turns the job of the Presidency over to the Military. *37350 Federal Register,*vol. 61, No. 138 / Wednesday, July 17, 1996 / Presidential Documents *16-18.*

National I.D. Card is here!

National Sunday law decree and National I.D. card can not be separated, the mark of the beast and the number of his name. Human activities will be controlled by the number. It will interconnect every human being to the World Wide Web. This will separate the Wheat from the Tares, the goats from the sheep. And the final movements will be rapid ones.

[Rev.17: 13-14 quoted] "In the warfare to be waged in the last days there will be united, in opposition to God's people, all the corrupt powers that have apostatized from the allegiance to the law of Jehovah. ***In this warfare the Sabbath of the fourth commandments will be the great point at issue:*** *for in the Sabbath commandment the great Lawgiver identifies Himself as the Creator of the heavens and the earth." — (MS 24, 1891)*

"And he causeth all, both small and great, rich and poor, free and bond, to receive a mark in their right hand, or in their foreheads: And that no man might buy or sell, save he that had the mark, or the name of the beast, or the number of his name. Here is wisdom. Let him that hath understanding count the number of the beast: for it is the number of a man; and his number [is] Six hundred threescore [and] six" —Rev. 13:16-18

Senate Passes Real ID: National ID Card On Its Way

- WASHINGTON, May 10 /U.S. Newswire -- House Judiciary Committee Chairman F. James Sensenbrenner, Jr. (R-Wis.), the author of the REAL ID Act (H.R. 418), issued the following statement following today's Senate passage of the supplemental appropriations conference report that included the REAL ID Act:
- Is this legislation a done deal?
Pretty much. The House of Representatives **approved the package on Thursday by a** vote of 368-58. Only three of the "nay" votes were Republicans; the rest were Democrats. The Senate is scheduled to vote on it next week and is expected to approve it as well.
- *U.S. Newswire, May 11,2005*
- ***The Senate has passed the Real ID bill, creating a backdoor national ID card****. After weeks of activism directed towards them, senators knew the full scale of this horror but voted for it 100-0 anyway.*
- So... When does it take effect?
The Real ID Act takes effect "**three years after the date of the enactment**" of the legislation. So if the Senate and Bush give it the thumbs-up this month, its effective date would be sometime in May 2008.

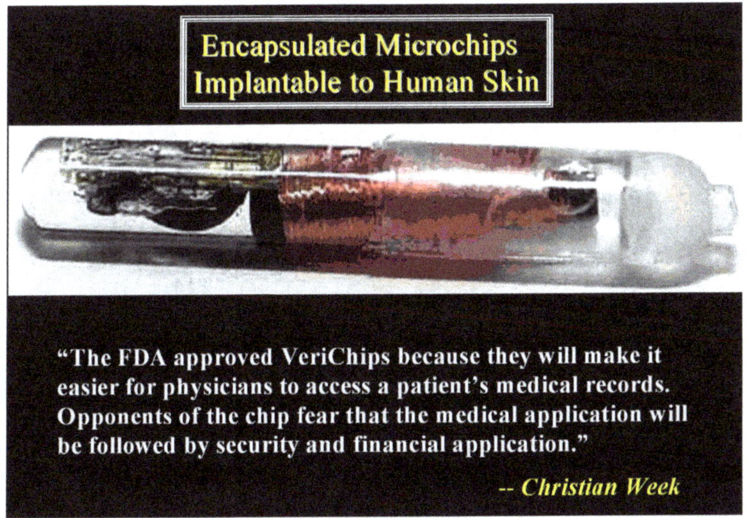

This is the first step towards receiving the mark of the beast. Article 12 says, **"The church shall unite on the day, Sunday according to the number."** The National I.D. Card will be used to impose economic boycott to God's people. You can not buy or sell without the number. The name or title of the beast is "vicarious filii dei" vicar of the son of God. The number of his name according to the Bible is the number of a man, and his number is 666. The final evolution of the I.D. Card will be in the form of micro chips to be implanted in human skin.

Final Warning to God's People

"A time is coming when the law of God is, in a special sense, to be made void in our land. The rulers of our nation will, by legislative enactments, enforce Sunday law, and thus ***God's people be brought into great peril.*** *When our nation, in its legislative councils, shall enact laws to bind the consciences of men in regard to their religious privileges, enforcing Sunday observance, and bringing oppressive power to bear against those who keep the seventh-day Sabbath, the law of God will, to all intents and purposes, be made void in our land; and* ***national apostasy will be followed by national ruin."*** *—Review & Herald, Dec. 18, 1888 {7BC 977.2}*

Greatest Light from Heaven-Greatest Peril and Darkness

America Can Become the Place of Greatest Peril

"America, . . . where the greatest light from heaven has been shining upon the people, can become the place of greatest peril and darkness because the people do not continue to practice the truth and walk in the light. . . ."
3 Selected Messages, 387

"The more nearly we approach the closing scenes of this earth's history, the more pronounced will be the work of Satan. Every species of deception will take the lead to divert the mind from God through Satan's devices."
--Letter 23c, 1894.

General Conference Bulletin 1901 : Outside United States every Seventh-day Adventist like to....

"The day is coming when every Seventh-day Adventist in the United States would give everything that he has if he could be outside of the United States. Let me say this again in speaking of something now that interest every Seventh-day Adventist. The day is coming and is not far off when every Seventh-day Adventist will wish to the depth of their soul that they were out of the United States, and multitude will condemn themselves and will fret themselves under the condemnation that they did not go out of the United States when they have chance."

- *Note: This quotation has been verified hanging on the wall of the library of the General Conference of Seventh-day Adventist."*

CHAPTER 9

REMNANT WILL ESCAPE

"And the ***remnant that is escaped*** *of the house of Judah shall again take root downward, and bear fruit upward; For* ***out of Jerusalem shall go forth a remnant****, and they that escaped out of mount Zion: the zeal of the LORD of hosts shall do this." —Isaiah 37:31-32*

Who is the Remnant?

"And the dragon was wroth with the woman (church), and went to make war with the remnant of her seed, which keep the commandments of God and have the testimony of Jesus Christ." —Rev. 12:17

"For the testimony of Jesus is the spirit of prophecy.". 19:10

"Esaias also crieth concerning Israel, Though the number of the children of Israel be as the sand of the sea, a remnant shall be saved." —Romans 9:27

"The remnant shall be very small and feeble." —Isaiah 16:4

"Enfeebled and defective as it may appear, the church is the one object upon which God bestows in a special sense His supreme regard." —Acts of the Apostles, p. 12

"The remnant of Israel shall do no iniquity nor speak lies, neither shall a deceitful tongue be found in their mouth." —Zephanaiah 3:13.

Who is God's True Church?

"Christ would have a church that labors to separate the evil from good, whose members will not willingly tolerate wrongdoing, but will expel it from the heart and life." — RH, Dec. 4, 1900

"From the beginning, faithful souls have constituted the church on earth." —Acts of the Apostles, p. 11

*"**God has a church.** It is not the great cathedral, neither is it the national establishment, neither is it the various denominations; it is the people who love God and keep His commandments.* ***'Where two or three are gathered***

together in my name, there am I in the midst of them *(Matt. 18:20). Where Christ is even among the humble few, this is Christ's church, for the presence of the High and Holy One who inhabiteth eternity can alone constitute a church." —Upward Look, p. 315*

"Now just as sure as the ***Philadelphian church is the true church of the last days****, just as sure the 144,000 are sealed, just before the coming of the Lord." —RH, May 9, 1854*

Apostles Meet in Home Church

- Romans 16:5 Likewise [greet] **the church that is in their house.** Salute my well beloved Epaenetus, who is the firstfruits of Achaia unto Christ.
- 1 Corinthians 16:19. The churches of Asia salute you. Aquila and Priscilla salute you much in the Lord, with **the church that is in their house.**
- Colossians 4:15 Salute the brethren which are in Laodicea, and Nymphas, and **the church which is in his house.**
- Philemon 1:2 And to [our] beloved Apphia, and Archippus our fellow soldier, and **to the church in thy house.**

WHO WILL BE ABLE TO ESCAPE?

Those Who Know Jesus Escape:

"For if after they have escaped the pollutions of the world through the knowledge of the Lord and Saviour Jesus Christ, they are again entangled therein, and overcome, the latter end is worse with them than the beginning.." —2 Peter 2:20

Those Who Genuinely Repent Escape:

"Yet will I leave a remnant that ye may have some that shall escape the sword among the nations, when ye shall be scattered through the countries. And they that escape of you shall remember me among the nations whither they shall be carried captives, because I am broken with their whorish heart, which hath departed from me, and with their eyes, which go a whoring after their idols: and they shall loathe themselves for the evils which they have committed in all their abominations." —Ezekiel 6:8-9

Those Who Watch and Pray Always Escape:
"Watch ye therefore, and pray always, that ye may be accounted worthy to escape all these things that shall come to pass, and stand before the Son of man." —Luke 31:36

Those Who Have Purified Themselves Escape:
"For then I will turn to the people a pure language that they may call upon the name of the Lord, to serve Him with one consent. The remnant of Israel shall do no iniquity, nor speak lies; neither shall a deceitful tongue be found in their mouth: for they feed and lie down, and none shall make them afraid." —Zephaniah 3:9, 13

Those Who Partake of the Divine Nature of God Escape:
"Whereby are given unto us exceeding great and precious promises: that by these ye might be partakers of the divine nature, having escaped the corruption that is in the world through lust." —2 Peter 1:4

WHO DO NOT ESCAPE?

Those Who Refuse to Hear and Yield to Jesus Cannot Escape:
"See that you refuse not Him that speaketh. For if they escaped not who refused Him that spake on earth, much more shall not we escape, if we turn away from Him that speaketh from heaven." —Hebrews 12:25

Those Who Reject the Prophets Escape Not:
"Ye serpents, ye generation of vipers, how can ye escape the damnation of hell? Wherefore, behold, I send unto you prophets, and wise men, and scribes: and some of them ye shall kill and crucify; and some of them shall ye scourge in your synagogues, and persecute them from city to city. That upon you may come all the righteous blood shed upon the earth, from the blood of righteous Abel unto the blood of Zacharias son of Barachias, whom ye slew between the temple and the altar." —Matthew 23:33-35

Those Who Preach Peace and Safety Shall not Escape
"For when they shall say, Peace and safety; then sudden destruction cometh upon them, as travail upon a woman with child; and they shall not escape." —1 Thessalonians 5:3

Those Who Neglect Salvation Do Not Escape
"How shall we escape, if we neglect so great salvation; which at the first began to be spoken by the Lord, and was confirmed unto us by them that heard Him." —Hebrews 2:3

Those Who Unjustly Judge and Criticize May Not Escape
"And thinkest thou this, O man, that judgest them which do such things, and does the same, that thou shalt escape the judgment of God?" —Romans 2:3

Unfaithful Shepherds and Ministers Will not Escape
"And the shepherds shall have no way to flee, nor the principal of the flock to escape." —Jeremiah 25:35

"I saw that the ministers did not escape the wrath of God. Their suffering was tenfold greater than that of their people." —Early Writings, p. 282

Where Did Our Leaders Get the Idea that the Laodicean SDA Church is the Translation Church?
"The (SDA) Laodicean church is the translation church… I have great consolation and gratitude in remembering that this is the very church that will be translated into the kingdom of God." —*By J. L. McElhany, president of the General Conference of SDA, Review and Herald, Nov. 30, 1939.* ***(Uninspired)***

Are We Saved Corporately, or Individually?
"The Seventh-day Adventist church will triumph gloriously and will go through triumphantly, ***as a corporate body****, to the sea of glass." — (From the well-known book "Early and the Latter Rain," used extensively by the SDA ministers and leaders worldwide, page 183.* ***[Uninspired].*** *The Bible says "work out your own salvation with fear and trembling."*

Salvation is Individual
"We are not saved as a sect; *no denominational name has any virtue to bring us into favor with God.* ***We are saved individually as believers in the Lord Jesus Christ****. And "by grace are ye saved through faith; and that not of yourselves; it is the gift of God." We may have our names recorded on the books of the most spiritual of the churches, and yet we may not belong to Christ, and our*

names may not be written on the Lamb's book of life." —2 Review and Herald, Feb. 10, 1891

How Many Will be Able to Escape?
There will be Few:

"And ye shall be left few in numbers, whereas ye were as stars of heaven for multitudes; because thou wouldest not obey the voice of the Lord thy God." —Deut. 28:62

"Esaias also crieth concerning Israel, Though the number of Israel be as the sand of the sea, a remnant shall be saved." —Romans 9:27.

"For many be called, but few are chosen." —Matthew 22:14.

"Because strait is the gate, and narrow is the way, which leadeth unto life, and few there be that find it." —Matthew 7:14

"Therefore hath the curse devoured the earth, and they that dwell therein are desolate: therefore the inhabitants of the earth are burned, and few men left." —Isaiah 24:6

"And said unto Jeremiah the prophet, Let, we beseech thee, our supplication be accepted before thee, and pray for us unto the LORD thy God, even for all this remnant; (for we are left but a few of many, as thine eyes do behold us)." —Jeremiah 42:2

"It is a solemn statement that I make to the church, that not one in 20 whose names are registered upon the church books are prepared to close their earthly history and who would be as verily without God and hope in the world as the common sinner." —Christian Service, p. 41

About One in Ten Come Through

"For thus saith the Lord GOD; The city that went out by a thousand shall leave an hundred, and that which went forth by an hundred shall leave ten, to the house of Israel." —Amos 5:3

Only a Few from Each Family Will Come Through

"Turn, O backsliding children, saith the LORD; for I am married unto you: and I will take you one of a city, and two of a family, and I will bring you to Zion." —Jeremiah 3:14

A Small Number Return

"Yet a small number that escape the sword shall return out of the land of Egypt into the land of Judah, and all the remnant of Judah that are gone into Egypt to sojourn there, shall know whose words shall stand, mine, or theirs." —Jeremiah 44:28

Who Were Gathered in Jerusalem?

"Son of man, the house of Israel is to me become a dross: all they are brass, and tin, and iron, and lead, in the midst of the furnace; they are even the dross of silver. Therefore thus saith the Lord GOD; because ye are all become dross, ***behold, therefore I will gather you into the midst of Jerusalem... Yea, I will gather you, and blow upon you in the fire of my wrath, and ye shall be melted in the midst thereof.*** *As the silver is melted in the midst of the furnace, so shall ye be melted in the midst thereof; and ye shall know that I the LORD have poured out my fury upon you." —Ezekiel 22:18-22*

What Will Happen to Modern Jerusalem (SDA)?

"Christ says, 'but I say unto you, it shall be more tolerable for Tyre and Sidon at the day of Judgment than for you. And thou Capernaum, [Seventh-day Adventist who have great light] which are exalted into heaven [in point of privilege], shalt be brought down to hell: for if the mighty works which have been done in thee had been done in Sodom it would have remained until this day. But I say unto you that it shall be more tolerable for the land of Sodom in the day of judgment than for thee." —3 Review & Herald, p. 69, Aug. 1, 1893

Who Gathered Them Out of Jerusalem?

"Jesus departed from Jerusalem, from the priests, the temple, the religious leaders, the people who had been instructed in the law, and turned to another class to proclaim His message, and ***gathered out*** *those who should carry the gospel to all nations." —Desire of Ages, p. 232*

"Fearing that the faith of the believers would be endangered by continued association with the opposers of the truth, Paul separated from them and ***gathered the disciples into a distinct body..."*** *—Acts of the Apostles, p. 286*

Who Will be Gathered Out of Modern Jerusalem and Who Will Gather Them?

"I saw that God has honest children among the nominal Adventist and the fallen churches, and before the plagues shall be poured out ministers and people will called out from these churches and will gladly receive the Truth. The light will shine and ***all who are honest will leave the fallen churches and take their stand with the remnant."*** *— Early Writings, p.261*

"The course pursued by those who hate the Truth will be the very means of opening the eyes of some. ***Every jewel will be brought out and gathered, for the hand of the Lord is set to recover the Remnant of his people."*** *—Early Writings, p.70*

Present Truth

"The truth is now to go forth with a power that it has not known for years. The message of ***PRESENT TRUTH*** *is to be proclaimed everywhere. The world must be prepared for the* ***Loud Cry of the Third Angel's message,*** *a message which God declares shall be cut short in righteousness." —Manuscript Releases Volume Ten, p. 218*

What is Present Truth?

"Therefore I will not be negligent to remind you always of these things, though you know them, and are established in the ***present truth****." —2 Peter 1:12*

"There are many precious truths that are contained in the Word of God but it is present truth that the flock needs now. I have seen the danger of the messengers running off from important points of present truth, to dwell upon subjects that are not calculated to unite the flock and sanctify the soul. Satan will here take every possible advantage to injure the cause.

But such subject as the sanctuary, in connection with the 2,300 days, the commandments of God and the faith of Jesus, are perfectly calculated to ***explain the past Advent movement and show what our present position is, establish the doubting, and give certainty to the glorious future.*** *These, I have frequently seen, were the principal subjects on which the messengers should dwell." —Early Writings, p. 63*

Present Sealing Truth

"The Lord has shown me that precious souls are starving, and dying for want of present sealing truth, the meat in due season; and the swift messengers should speed on their way, and feed the flock with present truth. I heard an Angel say, 'speed the swift messengers, speed the swift messengers; for the case of every soul will soon be decided, either for life or death." —Review & Herald, vol. 1, p. 11

Who Will be Gathered Out of Babylon?

"I saw another angel come down from heaven, having great power...And he cried mightily with a strong voice, saying, Babylon the great is fallen, is fallen... And I heard another voice from heaven, saying, ***Come out of her my people****, that ye be not partakers of her sins, and that ye receive not of her plagues.* ***For her sins have reached unto heaven,*** *and God hath remembered her iniquities." —Revelation 18:1-5*

When Do Her (Babylon) Sin Reach Unto Heaven?

"When do her (Babylon) sin reach unto heaven [Rev.18:1-5]? ***When the law of God is finally made void by legislation."*** *—LDE 198, (Signs of the Times, June 12, 1893)*

The When and Then of the Great Escape

"And the Saviour warned His followers: ***'When*** *ye therefore shall see the abomination of desolation spoken of by Daniel the prophet, stand in the holy place (whoso readeth let him understand),* ***then*** *let them which be in Judea flee into the mountains.' —Matthew 24:15,16* ***When*** *the idolatrous standards of the Romans (Vatican Flag) should be set up in the holy ground, which extended some furlongs outside the city walls,* ***then*** *the followers of Christ were to find safety in flight.*

"When *the warning signs should be seen, judgment was to follow so quickly that those who would escape must make no delay...* ***They must not hesitate a moment, lest they be involved in the general destruction."*** *—1884 G.C., p. 25-26*

As He Warned His Disciples...So He Has Warned His People Giving Them a Sign...

"Let men beware lest they neglect the lesson conveyed to them in the words of Christ. He has declared that He will

*come the second time, to gather his faithful ones to Himself, and to take vengeance of them that reject His mercy. As **He warned His disciples of Jerusalem's destruction,** giving them a sign of the approaching ruin that they might make their escape, **so He has warned His people** of the day of **final destruction**, and **giving them a sign** of its approach, that all who will may flee from the wrath to come." —1884 Great Controversy, p. 25*

Why Go Rather to Lost Sheep of the House of Israel (Modern Israel-SDA)?

*"As the apostles went forth with the good tidings of the kingdom, the Saviour's direction was, 'Go not into the way of the Gentiles, and into any city of the Samaritans enter ye not: **but go rather to the lost sheep of the house of Israel.'"** —Matthew 10:5, 6*

Judgment Must Begin at the House of God

"For the time [is come] that judgment must begin at the house of God: and if [it] first [begin] at us, what shall the end [be] of them that obey not the gospel of God?" —1 Peter 4:17

Since judgment will begin in the Seventh-day Adventist churches, it is only proper to give the warning to them. That is the objective of this small book.

SDA Church Weighed in the Balances of the Sanctuary

***"In the balances of the sanctuary the Seventh-day Adventist church is to be weighed**. She will be judged by the privileges and advantages that she has had. If her spiritual experience does not correspond to the advantages that Christ, at infinite cost, has bestowed on her, if the blessings conferred have not qualified her to do the work entrusted to her, on her will be pronounced the sentence: "Found wanting." By the light bestowed, the opportunities given, will she be judged." —Last Day Events, p. 59*

*"The Lord commissions His messengers [angels], the men with the slaughtering weapons in their hands: 'Go ye after him through the city, and smite: let not your eye spare, neither have ye pity: slay utterly old and young, both maids, and little children, and women: but come not near any man upon whom is the mark; **and begin at My sanctuary**. Then*

they began at the ancient men which were before the house' [Ezek 9:5-6]." —Testimonies, vol. 5, p 211

Betrayal of Remnant Seventh-day Adventist

"I saw the nominal churches and nominal Adventists, like Judas, ***would betray us to the Catholics*** *to obtain their influence to come against the truth.* ***The saints then will be an obscure people, little known to the Catholics;*** *but the churches and nominal Adventists who know of our faith and customs (for they hated us on account of the Sabbath, for they could not refute it will betray the saints and report them to the Catholics as those who disregard the institution of people; that is, that they keep the Sabbath and disregard Sunday." —Spalding and Magan, p. 1*

Stealthy Hands Slipping the Bolts

"These men who have been trusted to keep the fort have well-nigh betrayed it into the hands of the enemy. *They have opened the gates to a wily foe, who has sought to destroy them. Man of experience have seen stealthy hands slipping the bolts that Satan might enter; yet they held their peace with apparent indifference as to the results." —4 Testimonies, p. 211*

SDA Ministers Will Urge Upon SDA People to Keep Sunday

"The Lord has a controversy with His professed people in these last days. In this controversy, men in responsible positions will take a course directly opposite to that pursued by Nehemiah. They will not only ignore and despise the Sabbath themselves, but they will try to keep it from others by burying it beneath the rubbish of customs and tradition. In churches and in large gatherings in the open air, ***ministers will urge upon the people the necessity of keeping the first day of the week*** *(Sunday)." —1 Review and Herald, p. 405, (Mar. 18, 1884)*

God's Working Principles

"The Lord Jesus will always have a chosen people to serve Him. When the Jewish people rejected Christ, He took from them the kingdom of God and gave it to the Gentiles.

God will continue to work on these principles. *When the church proves unfaithful to the work of the Lord, whatever their position may be, however high and sacred their calling, the Lord can no longer work with them. Others are then chosen." — Upward Look, p. 131*

God Will Take the Reins in His Own Hands

"Let me tell you that the Lord will work in this last work in a manner very much out of the common order of things, and in a way that will be contrary to any human planning... God will use ways and means by which ***it will be seen that He is taking the reins in His own hands.****" —Testimonies to Ministers, p. 300*

Remnant Will Escapes Before Destruction

"And the ***remnant that is escaped*** *of the house of Judah shall again take root downward, and bear fruit upward; For* ***out of Jerusalem shall go forth a remnant....****"—Isaiah 37:31-32*

What Are God's Promises to Those Who Escape?

"The land of Judah had been laid waste by the army of occupation, but God had promised to provide miraculously for the needs of the people.... And ***the remnant that is escaped*** *of the house of Judah shall yet again take root downward, and bear fruit upward.* ***For out of Jerusalem***

***shall go forth a remnant**, and they that escape out of Mount Zion: the zeal of the Lord of host shall do this." —Prophets and Kings, p. 360*

"Watch ye therefore, and pray always, that ye may be accounted worthy to escape all these things that shall come to pass, and to stand before the Son of man." — Luke 21:34-36

CHAPTER 10

THE DESTRUCTION OF MODERN JERUSALEM

God loves His chosen people. Ancient Jerusalem/Israel was His chosen people in the time of Christ. But they disregarded His warnings and entreaties and walked in their own ways. They followed their human leader's teachings and own interpretation of the scriptures (the Sanhedrin, Rabbis, etc.) instead of following Jesus Christ as their leader. Their teachings, theology and creeds clashed with the teachings of Jesus. In the destruction of Jerusalem under the hands of the Romans, the remnant of Jerusalem, the true followers of Jesus were able to escape the destruction. Why? They watched for the promised sign and escaped to the mountains and were safe.

Consequently, God's last day chosen people, His modern Jerusalem/Israel (SDA) is, and will be experiencing the same fate as her predecessor. Two classes of people will emerge. One class will follow the Lamb whithersoever He goeth, the other will follow a strange shepherd—the deceiver.

"Satan's snares are laid for us as verily as they were laid for the children of Israel just prior to their entrance into the land of Canaan. We are repeating the history of that people. Lightness, vanity, love of ease and pleasure, selfishness, and impurity are increasing among us. There is need now of men who are firm and fearless in declaring the whole counsel of God; men who will not sleep as do others, but watch and be sober." —5 Testimonies, p.160

"In the seventeenth of Revelation is foretold the destruction of all churches who corrupt themselves by idolatrous devotion to the service of the papacy, those who have drunk of the wine of the wrath of her fornication. [Rev. 17:1-4 quoted]

"Thus is represented the papal power, which with all deceivableness of unrighteousness, by outside attraction and gorgeous display, ***deceives all nations****: promising them,*

as did Satan our first parents, all good to those who receive its mark, and all harm to those who oppose its fallacies." — (Letter 232, 1899), 7A SDA Bible Commentary

We are living in the most exciting period of this earth's history. Prophecies are fast fulfilling and points to the soon coming of our Lord and Saviour Jesus Christ. Pray to God to open the way for your escape from the destruction to come to this world.

"Before the destruction of Sodom, God sent a message to Lot, "Escape for thy life; look not behind thee, neither stay thou in all the plain; escape to the mountain, lest thou be consumed." The same voice of warning was heard by the Disciples of Christ before the destruction of Jerusalem: "When ye shall see Jerusalem compassed with armies, then, know that the desolation thereof is nigh. Then let them which are in Judea flee to the mountains." —Luke 21:20, 21 They must not tarry to secure anything from their possessions, but must make the most of the opportunity to escape.

***"There was a coming out, a decided separation from the wicked, an escape for life**. So it was in the days of Noah; so with Lot; so with the disciples prior to the destruction of Jerusalem; and so it will be in the last days. Again the voice of **God is heard in a message of warning, bidding His people separate themselves from the prevailing iniquity."** —Patriarchs and Prophets, p. 167*

Physical Jew Will Become Spiritual Jew

The orthodox Jews in Israel and in other parts of the world who are still keeping the Sabbath will be the object of the ire of Satan. Remember that they were the original chosen people. The Spiritual Israel (SDA) is only a grafted branch and should not be boastful of their spiritual standing. There are Jews around the world that had accepted Jesus Christ as their personal Saviour, and in the end both physical and spiritual Israel, those who are loyal to the commandments of God and the faith of Jesus will become one—the true Israel. The Spirit of Prophecy has something to say about physical Israel's end time role.

*"There will be **many converted from among the Jews**, and these converts will aid in preparing the way of the Lord*

and making straight in the desert a highway for our God. Converted Jews are to have an important part to act in the great preparations to be made in the future to receive Christ, our Prince." —Evangelism, p. 579

"There is a mighty work to be done in our world. The Lord has declared that the Gentiles shall be gathered in, and <u>*not the Gentiles only*</u>, ***BUT THE JEWS****. There are among the Jews many who will be converted, and through whom we shall see the salvation of God go forth as a lamp that burneth. There are Jews everywhere, and to them the light of* ***Present Truth*** *is to be brought. There are among them many who will come to the light, and who will proclaim the immutability of the Law of God with wonderful power. The Lord God will work. He will do wonderful things in righteousness." —Evangelism, p. 578*

Establishment of the State of Israel in May 14, 1948.

"And I will bring again the captivity of my people of Israel, and they shall build the waste cities, and inhabit [them]; and they shall plant vineyards, and drink the wine thereof; they shall also make gardens, and eat the fruit of them.

"And I will plant them upon their land, and they shall no more be pulled up out of their land which I have given them, saith the LORD thy God." —Amos 9:14-15

On May 14, 1948, on the day in which the British Mandate over a Palestine expired, the Jewish People's Council gathered at the Tel Aviv Museum, and approved the following proclamation, declaring the establishment of the State of Israel. The new state was recognized that night by the United States and three days later by the USSR.

There are Jews around the world who had accepted Jesus Christ as their personal Saviour. Not all Jews have rejected Jesus the Son of God. They have experienced terrible things during their 70 year captivity in the hands of the Babylonians. They suffered persecution and destruction in the hands of the Romans in 70 A.D. They suffered persecution and destruction in the hands of Hitler during the holocaust. And even now, they are so hated and persecuted by their neighboring Arab nations. Why are they so hated by the world? They are not bad people, they are not terrorists. Many might not be aware of this, but I personally believe that the orthodox Jews are still the symbol of God's commandment keeping people. Most of Jews are Sabbath keepers, particularly the Orthodox Jews and the Christian Jews. Satan hates the Seventh-day Sabbath because in it is contained the seal of the living God. The Sabbath is the sign of God's Creatorship and Lordship. *"Therefore the Son of man is Lord also of the Sabbath." —Mark 2:28*

Modern Israel (SDA)—the spiritual Israel will suffer intense persecution and destruction under the hands of the Papacy and Protestantism combined, as predicted in the Bible and Spirit of Prophecy. Don't be fooled by the ecumenical "Trojan Horse" of the Papacy—the World Council of Churches. Rome has not changed. She is patiently waiting for a vantage ground and it will strike like a venomous scorpion.

"The Christian world will learn what Romanism really is, when it is too late to escape the snare. She is silently growing into power. Her doctrines are exerting their influence in legislative halls, in the churches, and in the hearts of men. Throughout the land she is piling up her lofty and massive structures, in the secret recesses of which **her former persecutions will be repeated.** *She is stealthily*

and unsuspectedly strengthening her forces to further her own ends when the time shall come for her to strike. All that she desires is vantage ground, and this is soon to be given her. In the near future we shall see and shall feel what the purpose of the Roman element is. ***Whoever shall believe and obey the word of God will thereby incur reproach and persecution.*** *<4SP 397.2>*

Remember Saint Bartholomew's Day Massacre

*"**But blackest in the black catalogue of crime**, most horrible among the fiendish deeds of all the dreadful centuries, was the St. Bartholomew Massacre. The world still recalls with shuddering horror the scenes of that most cowardly and cruel onslaught.* ***The king of France, urged on by Romish priests and prelates, lent his sanction to the dreadful work.*** *A bell, tolling at dead of night, was a signal for the slaughter. Protestants by thousands, sleeping quietly in their homes, trusting to the plighted honor of their king, were dragged forth without a warning and murdered in cold blood. {GC 272.1}*

"The papal church will never relinquish her claim to infallibility. All that she has done in her persecution of those who reject her dogmas, she holds to be right; and would she not repeat the same acts, should the opportunity

be presented? ***Let the restraints now imposed by secular governments be removed, and Rome be re-instated in her former power, and there would speedily be a revival of her tyranny and persecution.*** *<4SP 381.2>*

Last Days Warfare

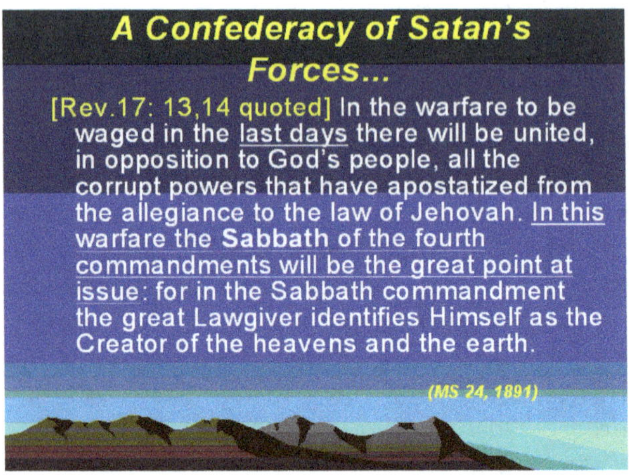

Vatican is symbolized by the woman of Revelation 17
"And the woman which thou sawest is that great city, which reigneth over the kings of the earth." —Revelation 17:18

"In the issue of the great contest, two distinct opposite classes developed. *One class "worship the beast and*

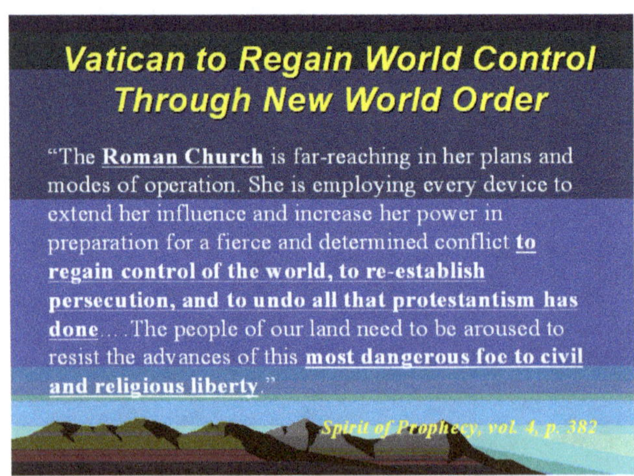

his image, and receive his mark," and thus bring upon themselves the awful judgments threatened by the third angel. The other class in marked contrast to the world, "keep the commandments of God and the faith of Jesus." —Revelation 14: 9-12

Claiming to be the vicar of the Son of God, it has been his long time ambition to have his palace moved to Jerusalem. The Mohammedans were used by the Papacy to conquer Jerusalem for his glory. But after Jerusalem was conquered, the Mohammedans reneged on their promise and built their shrine instead—the Dome of the Rock. It is considered holy second to Mecca. Surprisingly, Ex-Prime Minister Simon Peres of Israel offered to hand over the sovereignty of Jerusalem's Old City to the Vatican, and even PLO leader Yasser Arafat agreed to it.

One of the Jewish Biblical Scholar believes that there is but one prophecy in the Bible that is not fulfilled. He quoted Zechariah 12:2. ***"Behold, I will make Jerusalem a cup of trembling unto all the people round about****, when they shall be in the siege both against Judah [and] against Jerusalem."* He said that the whole world under the Papal New World Order will battle against Israel and then Messiah would come.

"Behold, the day of the LORD cometh, and thy spoil shall be divided in the midst of thee. ***For I will gather all***

Vaticanization of Old City of Jerusalem

- "Simon Peres [Ex-Prime Minister of Israel] offered to hand over sovereignty of Jerusalem's Old City to the Vatican. Jerusalem is to stay as the Capital of Israel but, the Old City will be administered by the Vatican."
- "The PLO was shown the Vaticanization Plan just before the signing of the Declaration of Principles. At that time Arafat agreed not to oppose the plan. Arafat consulted with a number of influencial Palestinians who were delighted with the plan. The plan called for the extra-territoriality of the Old City and the airport Atarot, which would become a world-wide meeting center."
- "The Italian newspaper *La Stampa* on Sept.10, 1993, published the plan. Further details of the plan claim Jerusalem is to become the **second Vatican of the world** with three major religions represented under the authority of the Vatican."

The Jews and Jerusalem, by Vance Ferrell.

nations against Jerusalem to battle; *and* ***the city shall be taken****, and the houses rifled, and the women ravished; and half of the city shall go forth into captivity, and the residue of the people shall not be cut off from the city." —Zechariah 14:1-2*

"And the ten horns which thou sawest are ten kings, which have received no kingdom as yet; but receive power as kings ***one hour*** *with the beast.* ***These have one mind, and shall give their power and strength unto the beast."*** *—Rev. 17:12-13*

According to Gary Kah, author of "Enroute to Global Occupation" the whole world is now divided into 10 regions under the New World Order. As the Bible prophesied, the whole world will unite for one hour (Biblical one hour equals 14 days) and surrender their sovereignty to the N.W.O. The woman riding the beast represents the Papacy, who will be leading the political, economic, and religious boycott against God's remnant people in the last days of this earth's history.

Three Major World Religions Occupy Old Jerusalem

Now that the Old City of Jerusalem has been handed down to the control of Vatican without the use of force or conquest,

"he shall plant his tabernacle of his palace between the seas in the glorious holy mountains;" —Daniel 11:45

As Administrator of Old Jerusalem, he will build his tabernacle in the glorious holy mountain of Jerusalem ***"so that he as God sitteth in the temple of God, showing himself that he is God."*** *—2 Thessalonians, 2:4,* and as predicted it will be called **second Vatican of the world**. Finally, after so many centuries have passed, he will now have fulfilled his long time aspiration to sit in the temple of God in Jerusalem, showing himself that he is God—the anti-Christ.

The whole world united politically, economically and religiously under the N.W.O. will be at war with Jesus the Lamb of God, together with his faithful servants, those who keep the commandments of God and the faith of Jesus. They are at war because they will make void the Law of God, and enforce a spurious Sunday sabbath under penalty of death. But before Satan can wipe out God's people, He will come to rescue them. ***"Behold, I come quickly;*** *and my reward [is] with me, to give every man according as his work shall be." —Revelation 22:12*

The Good News—Jesus is Coming!

"These shall make war with the Lamb, and the Lamb shall overcome them: for He is the Lord of lords, and King of kings: and they that are with Him are called and chosen and faithful." —Rev. 17:14. At the second coming of Jesus, He will change from His high priestly robe and put on His kingly garment, throwing down the censer with lightning and thundering, He will say "It is finished." This is the second coming of Jesus in the clouds of glory. He will then deliver His called, and chosen and faithful servants from total enslavement under Satan's New World Order.

FINAL WARNING—FALL OF N.W.O.

"And after these things I saw another angel come down from heaven, having great power; and the earth was lightened with his glory.

"And he cried mightily with a strong voice, saying, Babylon the great is fallen, is fallen, and is become the habitation of devils, and the hold of every foul spirit, and a cage of every unclean and hateful bird.

"For all nations have drunk of the wine of the wrath of her fornication, and the kings of the earth have committed fornication with her, and the merchants of the earth are waxed rich through the abundance of her delicacies." — Rev.18:1-3

COME OUT OF HER MY PEOPLE!

"And I heard another voice from heaven, saying, ***Come out of her, my people,*** *that ye be not partakers of her sins, and that ye receive not of her plagues." —Rev 18:4*

Many Not in Our Ranks to Come to the Front

"There are many souls to come out of the ranks of the world, out of the churches—even the Catholic Church—whose zeal will far exceed that of those who have stood in rank and file to proclaim the truth heretofore. For this reason the eleventh hour laborers will receive their penny. These will see the battle coming and will give the trumpet a certain sound. When the crisis is upon us, when the season of calamity shall come, they will come to the front, gird themselves with the whole armor of God, and exalt His law, adhere to the faith of Jesus, and maintain the cause of religious liberty which reformers defended with toil and for which they sacrificed their lives. . . ." —3 Selected Messages 386

NATIONAL SUNDAY LAW PASSED

"For her sins have reached unto heaven, *and God hath remembered her iniquities." —Rev. 18:5*

"When do her (Babylon) sin reach unto heaven? [Rev. 18:5]? ***When the law of God is finally made void by legislation."*** *—Last Days Event, p.198, Signs of the Times, 6/12/1893*

Persecution by Protestants and Popery Combined

"A spurious sabbath is presented to be legislated into power, compelling the observance of a sabbath which God has not enjoined upon man. ***The persecutions of Protestants by Romanism, by which the religion of Jesus Christ was almost annihilated, will be more than rivaled, when Protestantism and popery are combined.*** *. . ." —3 Selected Messages, p. 387*

America Can Become the Place of Greatest Peril

"America, . . . where the greatest light from heaven has been shining upon the people, can become the place of greatest peril and darkness because the people do not continue to practice the truth and walk in the light . . .. —3 SM 387

"The more nearly we approach the closing scenes of this earth's history, the more pronounced will be the work of Satan. Every species of deception will take the lead to divert the mind from God through Satan's devices." —Letter 23c, 1894

The Mother of Harlots and Abominations

"Reward her even as she rewarded you, and double unto her double according to her works: in the cup which she hath filled fill to her double.

"How much she hath glorified herself, and lived deliciously, so much torment and sorrow give her: for she saith in her heart, ***I sit a queen, and am no widow, and shall see no sorrow.*** *" —Rev. 18:6-7*

The woman of Revelation 17 riding the beast of the New World Order is so boastful that she sits as queen. She, being the woman riding the scarlet colored beast, on her forehead is written, MYSTERY, BABYLON THE GREAT, THE MOTHER OF HARLOTS AND ABOMINATIONS OF THE EARTH, will suffer judgment from the Creator God, together with the kings of the earth—the political leaders of various nations who have conspired with her, and also, the merchants of the earth—the religious leaders of various denominations who have deceived millions of souls into believing that the law of God is no longer valid, especially they made void the Sabbath of the fourth commandment.

JUDGMENT OF GOD

"Therefore shall her plagues come in one day, death, and mourning, and famine; and she shall be utterly burned with fire: for strong [is] the Lord God who judgeth her.

"And the kings of the earth, who have committed fornication and lived deliciously with her, shall bewail her, and lament for her, when they shall see the smoke of her burning,

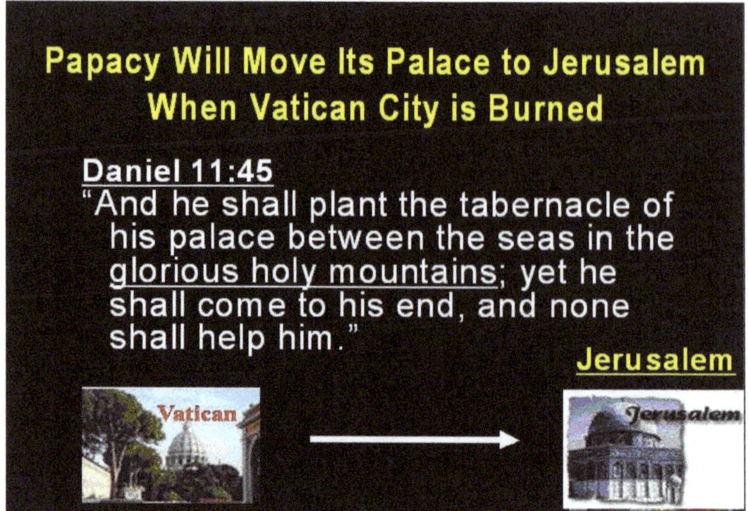

"Standing afar off for the fear of her torment, saying, Alas, alas that great city Babylon, that mighty city! For in one hour is thy judgment come.

"And the merchants of the earth shall weep and mourn over her; for no man buyeth their merchandise any more:

"The merchandise of gold, and silver, and precious stones, and of pearls, and fine linen, and purple, and silk, and scarlet, and all thyine wood, and all manner vessels of ivory, and all manner vessels of most precious wood, and of brass, and iron, and marble,

"And cinnamon, and odours, and ointments, and frankincense, and wine, and oil, and fine flour, and wheat, and beasts, and sheep, and horses, and chariots, ***and slaves, and souls of men.****" —Revelation 18:8-13*

Have you noticed their merchandise? It's astonishing! It includes slaves and souls of men. They made religion a big business by enslaving people with their dogmas and doctrines.

"But in vain they do worship me, teaching [for] doctrines the commandments of men." —Matthew 15:9

"The merchants of these things, which were made rich by her, *shall stand afar off for the fear of her torment, weeping and wailing, And saying, Alas, alas, that great city, that was clothed in fine linen, and purple, and scarlet, and decked* *with gold, and precious stones, and pearls! For in one hour so great riches is come to nought. And every shipmaster, and all the company in ships, and sailors, and as many as trade by sea, stood afar off,* ***And cried when they saw the smoke of her burning, saying, What [city is] like unto this great city!*** *And they cast dust on their heads, and cried, weeping and wailing, saying, Alas, alas, that great city, wherein were made rich all that had ships in the sea by reason of her costliness!* ***for in one hour is she made desolate****. Rejoice over her, [thou] heaven, and [ye] holy apostles and prophets; for* ***God hath avenged you on her.****" —Revelation 18:15-20*

The Bible says that under the New World Order, they will unite for a short space of time [Rev. 17:10]. *"And the ten horns which thou sawest upon the beast, these shall hate the whore, and shall make her desolate and naked, and shall eat her flesh, and burn her with fire." —Rev.* 17:16 Like what Nero did in the past, when he burned Rome and blamed it on the Christians, the burning of Vatican will also be blamed on the faithful followers of Christ who keep the Seventh-day Sabbath.

GOD DELIVERS HIS PEOPLE

"God would not suffer the wicked to destroy those who were expecting translation; and who would not bow to the decree of the beast or receive his mark. I saw that if the wicked were permitted to slay the saints, Satan and all his evil host, and all who hate God, would be gratified. And oh, what a triumph it would be for his satanic majesty, to have power, in the last closing struggle, over those who had so long waited to behold Him whom they loved! Those who have mocked at the idea of the saints' going up will witness the care of God for His people, and behold their glorious deliverance." —EW 284 (1858) Last Day Events, p. 263

"And when these things begin to come to pass, then look up, and lift up your heads; for your redemption draweth nigh." —Luke 21:28

Signs by Land and Sea (From Faith I Live By)

"The great day of the Lord is near, it is near, and hasteth greatly*, even the voice of the day of the Lord: the mighty man shall cry there bitterly." —Zeph. 1:14*

"**We are near the close of time.** *I have been shown that the retributive judgments of God are already in the land. The Lord has given us warning of the events about to take place. . . . Those who are drinking from the same fountain of blessing will draw nearer together. Truth dwelling in the hearts of believers will lead to blessed and happy assimilation. Thus will be answered the prayer of Christ that His disciples might be one even as He is one with the Father. For this oneness every truly converted heart will be striving.*

"With the ungodly there will be a deceptive harmony that but partially conceals a perpetual discord. **In their opposition to the will and the truth of God they are united,** *while on every other point they are rent with hatred, emulation, jealousy, and deadly strife.*

"The Lord is removing His restrictions from the earth, *and soon there will be death and destruction, increasing crime, and cruel, evil working against the rich who have exalted themselves against the poor.* **Those who are without God's protection will find no safety in any place or position.** *Human agents are being trained and are using their inventive power to put into operation the most powerful machinery to wound and to kill.*

"The Lord will arise to shake terribly the earth. *We shall see troubles on all sides. Thousands of ships will be hurled into the depths of the sea. Navies will go down, and human lives will be sacrificed by millions.* ***Fires will break out unexpectedly, and no human effort will be able to quench them. The palaces of earth will be swept away in the fury of the flames. Disasters by rail will become more and more frequent; confusion, collision, and death without a moment's warning will occur on the great lines of travel. The end is near, probation is closing. Oh, let us seek God while He may be found, call upon Him while He is near!" —FLB343***

ASPECT
Books

www.ingramcontent.com/pod-product-compliance
Lightning Source LLC
LaVergne TN
LVHW050539100826
845148LV00002B/614

9781572585461